FAMILIAR VOICES

GU00496972

Frank Harbord

Able Publishing

FAMILIAR VOICES

Published by
Able Publishing
13 Station Road, Knebworth
Herts. SG3 6AP
Tel: 01438 814316 Fax: 01438 815232

About the title & the front cover.

The Aircraft pictured at the top of the front cover is the Duxford restored Mk.IV Blenheim painted in the colours of the aircraft flown by W/C. H.I. Edwards on 'operation wreckage', a daylight raid on Bremen in July 1941. For this exploit the W/C was awarded the Victoria Cross.

This photograph reproduced with the kind permission of Mr. John Smith, The Aeroplane Restoration Company, Duxford Airfield, Cambridgeshire.

The aircraft in the bottom picture is a Fairey "Battle" as used for air-firing practice at Aldergrove in 1939. See caption under similar photograph at front of Chapter three.

The book title is taken from the poem "In Memoriam" written by Ron Johnson of 223 Sqdn. while he was P.O.W. in early 1945. His life was saved by bailing out of his stricken aircraft at night from over twenty thousand feet. Six other crew members died.

This poem, amongst others, was read out to the congregation at the dedication of the memorial stone at Oulton, Norfolk, in May 1994. The stone commemorates all those airmen of all nationalities who lost their lives while flying from the R.A.F. station at Oulton.

The memorial stone was unveiled by Air Vice Marshal Jack Furner, C.B.E., O.B.E., D.F.C., A.F.C..

For the poem "In Memoriam" see following page.

This poem is dedicated to the six members of the crew of Liberator J Johnnie of 223 Squadron killed when our aircraft was shot down over Germany on the night of 20/21 February 1945.

IN MEMORIAM

Who loved life
Just as much as I
Nor wished to fight
Or fighting wished to die
How shall I tell of you my friends?
What songs shall satisfy

My heart? What verses
Penetrate the crowd
Of platitudes when crude
Pen-scribblings shroud
With drooping laurels your simple dignity
The stars were lost in cloud

The night I left you
Four miles high
Above the German mountains
Falling from the sky
Like flaming Autumn leaves
There was no time to say goodbye

Familiar voices heard
Above the engines roar
Our flying kit flung carelessly
Across the crewroom floor
Are murals for my inner walls
Point, counterpoint of war

And so for me
You did not die
Because the corn grew tall
Where you passed by
And you loved living
Every bit as much as I

RWJ
June 1945

Best wishes
Ron Johnson.

Rx RAF FL/LT NAVIGATOR
223 Squadron

INTRODUCTION

This book is the story of the author's involvement with 'D' Company, 4th Battalion, Lincolnshire Regiment, T.A. and the Royal Air Force between May 1936 and December 1947. It is written from memory more than fifty years after the events related.

The book is not intended to be a work of reference for the serious historian, just a day to day account of typical happenings that occurred in those days; written for the enlightenment of my children, grand-children, other relatives and friends, old comrades and any other interested reader.

Members of my family have suggested from time to time over many years that my experiences should be written down. These suggestions I rejected, sometimes gruffly. With the passing of the years and with prodding, encouragement and smooth words from family and friends outside the family I have now put pen to paper.

The period of history covered by each chapter, the locations and the units/squadrons involved, maps etc. are listed on the title sheet of each chapter.

Photographs, maps, diagrams etc. pertaining to that chapter are printed between the title sheet of the chapter and the beginning of the narrative. This arrangement ensures the reader knows of their where-abouts when they are needed to clarify and round out the text.

Where a map is referred to in more than one chapter, the title sheet of the later chapters will give the number of the map and the number of the chapter where first used.

" ... Old men forget; yet all shall be forgot ..."
(King Henry the Fifth, Act IV, Scene III)

The author would be pleased to hear from anyone who can correct any misconceptions or memory failures.

Frank Harbord
Welwyn Garden City, 1998

Further reading

Title	Author
Valiant Wings.	Norman Franks
Battle Axe Blenheims	Stuart R. Scott
Solvitur Ambulando	Eric Moss
Low Level from Swanton Morley	Martin Bowman
God is My Co-Pilot	Colonel Scott
R.A.F. Great Massingham	Peter B. Gunn
Malta Convoy.	Shankland & Hunter

Dedication

This book is dedicated to all who served in the armed forces of the crown during those desperate days of World War II, particularly that officer and gentleman Wing Commander Sidney John Monroe, D.F.C., killed on active service 29th October 1942.

He who knows all understands and forgives all.
(With apologies to Blaise Pascal, 1623-1662)

ACKNOWLEDGEMENTS

My thanks are due to:
S/L Don McLeod, R.A.F. (Ret'd.)

W/O Eric Moss, R.A.F. (Ret'd.)

F/L George Paul, R.A.F. (Ret'd.)
    Now of Imperial War Museum, Duxford

Ex-Army L/Cpl. Iolo Lewis
    3rd Royal Tank Regt., 1941-1947
    President, Welwyn Garden City Branch,
    Royal British Legion.

S/L D.W. (Joe) Warne, R.A.F. (Ret'd.)

Royal Air Force Museum, Hendon.

F/Sgt. Margaret Dwerryhouse, W.A.A.F. (Ret'd.)

Mr Julian Horne and Mr Paul Lincoln
    Wartime Watton Museum.

Air Marshal Sir Ivor Broom KCB. CBE. DSO. DFC. AFC. for the
foreword

Members of my Family.

Members of the local branches of the R.A.F.A., The Royal British
Legion and The Burma Star Association.

And many more who have helped, often unknowingly, by kind words
of encouragement and approval.

Foreword by
Air Marshal Sir Ivor Broom
KCB., CDE., DSO., DFC., AFC.,

Frank Harbord's service to his country started in the Territorial Army at the age of 18. This was followed by volunteering for aircrew duties in the Royal Air Force in 1939 when war seemed imminent. Between July 1939 and December 1947 he gave great service to his country as an air observer in a wide variety of operational tasks. This book covers his memories of those days which were so critical for the future of our nation. Memories of recent days by most people are often fickle and distorted but I find that memories of events 50 or 60 years ago are invariably accurate and vivid in the memories of men who served in the Armed Forces in World War 2.

Having joined the Royal Air Force in 1939 he was actively engaged in 1940 in attacks on channel ports and enemy shipping - probably the most critical year in our recent history. Like Frank Harbord I took part in Blenheim operations from East Anglia and Malta in 1941 and his memories of those days accord precisely - often in great detail - with my own. The very low level attacks on shipping and coastal targets, the heavy losses, the sudden loss of friends, the damage to aircraft - all were accepted as facts of life.

continued over leaf.

continued from previous page.

Operations in Europe were followed by four varied years of service in the Middle East, India and Burma including a short spell as a "Flying Control Officer" the name given to air traffic controllers in those days. In 1947 he retired from the Royal Air Force after packing into those eight years in the service a remarkable lifetime of experience. It is good that this story has been recorded for posterity.

IVOR BROOM

6 APRIL 1999

CONTENTS

CHAPTER ONE

LIFE BEFORE THE RAF
(THE 1920s AND 1930s)

*FOR LOCATION OF PLACES REFERRED TO IN THIS
CHAPTER SEE MAP No.1.*

List of illustrations etc. at the beginning of chapter 1.

Map No. 1.
Extract from "The Aeroplane" of June 22nd 1927
Sketch of "Hucks" starter
Notes on "Hucks" starter
Ceremonial Parade at Haltwhistle (Northumberland) August 1936
Marching into camp at Beverley (Yorks.) August 1937
No. 14 Platoon, Halton (Lancashire) August 1938
Notes on above photograph
Major G S Jones, D.S.O.
Airspeed "Ferry" and Hawker "Hart"
Drawing of Sopwith "Snipe"
Hucks starter of the Shuttleworth Collection at Old Warden aerodrome
September 1998.

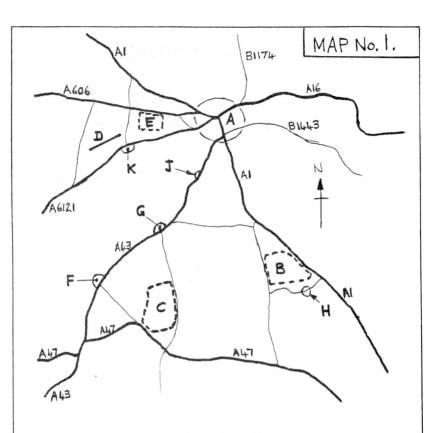

OUTLINE MAP OF THE **STAMFORD** AREA, RAILWAYS, RIVER WELLAND & MINOR ROADS OMITTED FOR CLARITY. SCALE APPROX 0 — 1 MILE — 2 MILES.

A. STAMFORD TOWN.
B. WITTERING AERODROME.
C. EASTON-ON-THE-HILL/COLLYWESTON AERODROME.
D. RIFLE BUTTS AT TINWELL.
E. FIELDS USED AS LANDING GROUND BY FLYING CIRCUSES.
F. COLLYWESTON VILLAGE.
G. EASTON-ON-THE-HILL VILLAGE.
H. WITTERING VILLAGE.
J. SITE OF AEROPLANE CRASH IN JUNE 1927.
K. TINWELL VILLAGE.

Extract from "The Aeroplane" of June 22nd, 1927.
Page 724

A Fatal Accident

The Air Ministry regrets to announce that as the result of an accident at Stamford to a Sopwith Snipe of the Central Flying School, Wittering, on June 16th. Flt Lt Humphrey William Baggs, the pilot of the aircraft, and Flg Off Sidney Fleetwood Bell, were killed.

* * * * * *

Information on the 'Snipe' aircraft from other sources:

About 2,000 'Snipe' aircraft were built between the beginning of 1918 and 1923. The engine was a 230 h.p. Bentley Rotary type BR2.

About 40 'Snipe' aircraft were built as two-seaters for pilot training, the remainder being single seater fighters.

Site of crash marked 'J' on map no. 1.

* * * * * *

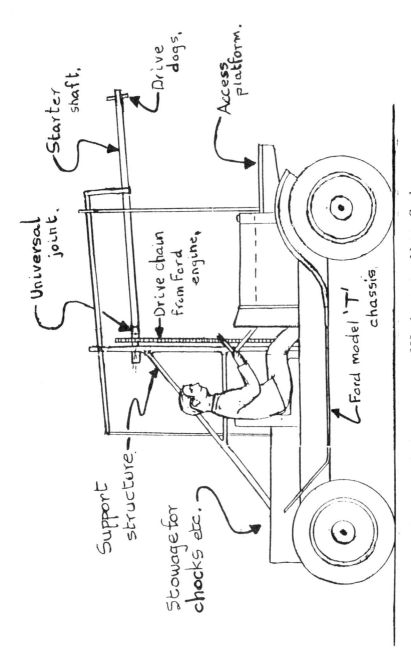

Starter shaft.

Drive dogs.

Access platform.

Universal joint.

Drive chain from Ford engine.

Support structure.

Stowage for chocks etc.

Ford model 'T' chassis.

Diagrammatic Arrangement of Hucks starter. Not to Scale.
See notes on page 15 and photograph on page 28.

14

THE HUCKS STARTER
(See sketch on page 14.)

The starter was driven up to face the aircraft to be started, leaving a gap of about four to five feet. A mechanic then standing on the access platform could lift the forward end of the starter shaft from its rest, extend it forward and engage the dogs in the corresponding hooks on the aircraft propellor boss.

Torque supplied by the starter engine could then be applied to the starter shaft which in turn rotated the aircraft propellor to start the aircraft engine.

When the aircraft engine fired the drive dogs were thrown out of engagement with the propellor and the starter shaft retracted to fall back into its rest position.

The starter, its purpose fulfilled, was then driven away.

Ceremonial Parade

138th Infantry Brigade, Haltwhistle, Northumberland, August 1936

'D' Company, 4th Battalion, Lincolnshire Regiment, T.A. marching into camp at Beverly, Yorkshire, August 1937
Frank Harbord is fourth from the left in the column nearest the camera

17

14 Platoon, 'D' Company, 4th Battallion, Lincolnshire Regiment, T.A.

These notes apply to the photograph on page 18.

The photograph was taken whilst the Battallion was at annual camp at Halton, Lancashire, in August 1938.

Front row, seated, from the left:

2nd. the red sash worn by this (unknown) soldier indicates some official 24 hour duty.
3rd. the red sash indicates Orderly Sergeant for the day.
4th. Major G.S. Jones, wearing his First World War medals, the Company Commander
5th. 1st Lieutenant Peter Blackstone, the 2 i/c. He is holding the Brownlow Cup awarded to the Platoon for efficiency.
6th. Sergeant Jack Pollack, the Platoon sergeant.
Back row, standing, on the right, Harry Pickett, next to him Frank Harbord.
The four boys sitting on the ground in the front are doing boys service, under 18s.
The Brownlow Cup is now preserved, with other town silver, in the Town Hall, at Stamford.

Rutland & Stamford Mercury, Friday, May 11, 1990

Major's bravery at Dunkirk

The nation is gearing up to mark the 50th anniversary of the British Army's retreat at Dunkirk.

But did you know that a Stamford dentist played a major role in the events of June 1 and 2?

The research of Lincoln historian Roy Vernon has unearthed details of the bravery of Major Gilbert Sidney Jones of the 6th Battalion Lincolnshire Regiment, who won a DSO for his help in evacuating the beaches.

Major Jones stood up to his chest in

Major Gilbert Sidney Jones DSO.

water, and under heavy shell fire assisted exhausted soldiers into the boats.

He lived at 59 St Martin's and died in 1959, aged 66.

Major G. S. Jones, D.S.O.
Reproduced courtesy "Rutland & Stamford Mercury".

The above photograph shows a Hawker "Hart" of No. 11 F.T.S. climbing away just after take-off from the R.A.F. aerodrome at Wittering in November 1935.

The aircraft shown in the above photograph is the Airspeed "Ferry" of Sir Alan Cobham's Flying Circus which visited Stamford in 1936.

Both the above photographs were taken by the writer using the most elementary box camera as were commonly in use at that time.

SOPWITH AVIATION Co. LTD.   SNIPE 7 F.I.   1918.

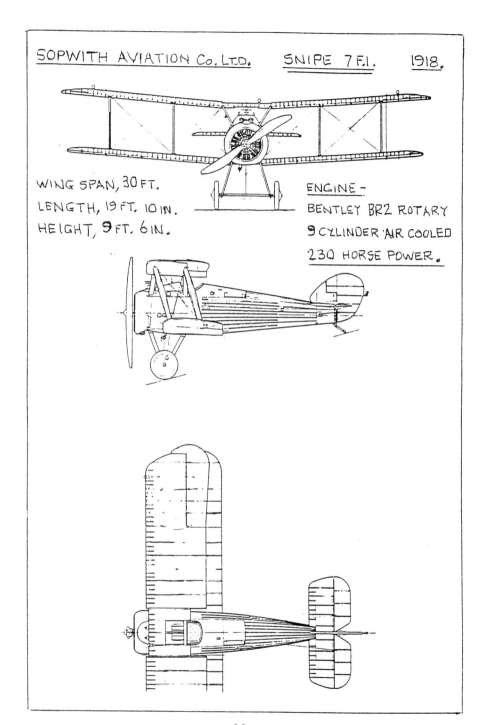

WING SPAN, 30 FT.
LENGTH, 19 FT. 10 IN.
HEIGHT, 9 FT. 6 IN.

ENGINE –
BENTLEY BR2 ROTARY
9 CYLINDER AIR COOLED
230 HORSE POWER.

My arrival in the world was about two months before the end of WW1. During WW1 the Royal Flying Corps had used an aerodrome situated about two miles south of Stamford (Lincs) on the west side of the old Great North Road (now the A1) and just to the north of the village of Wittering. This aerodrome became known as Wittering. My parents lived to the north of Stamford during the 1920's and 1930's and I went to school in Stamford.

After WW1 the RAF moved out of Wittering and the wartime camp was left dis-used. About 1923 it was decided that the aerodrome at Wittering was needed as a permanent base for units of the RAF and construction work started on permanent buildings on the site.

In 1926 the aerodrome at Wittering was re-opened and the Central Flying School moved in from Upavon (Wilts). To the boys in Stamford, creeping unwillingly to school, it seemed that aeroplanes from Wittering were always overhead performing aerobatics, practising forced landings and similar manoeuvres. It appeared that an airman's life was one of complete freedom, full of excitement.

As well as the aerodrome at Wittering in WW1, the Royal Flying Corps had another aerodrome about three miles to the west of Wittering known as Easton-on-the-Hill to the RFC, the name being changed to Collyweston in 1918 when the RAF was formed. This aerodrome remained in use after WW1 until it was decided to build a permanent aerodrome at Wittering in 1923, the aerodrome at Collyweston was then abandoned.

During the summer holidays from school half-a-dozen of us ten to twelve year old boys would cycle up to the now disused WW1 aerodrome at Easton-on-the-Hill/Collyweston. Here we would just wander about where the old camp had been and where the concrete floors of the huts still remained. Round about these areas of concrete, amongst the long grass and stinging nettles we would pick out bits of wood with metal fittings that to our imaginations were remnants of wartime aircraft.

We would also cycle about to support the village cricket team when they played the surrounding villages. One dinner time at school an aeroplane came over the school lower than usual with its engine banging and giving out smoke. It went down behind the houses. Those of us who had bikes set off in the direction it was heading to see if it had come down. Our senses were right, it had come down and the wreckage was tangled up in the hedgerow at the side of the Wothorpe Road about a mile and a half south/south-west of Stamford. As we arrived the two occupants were being taken away in an ambulance.

Other aircraft landed in the field and took off again, it was the first time we had seen aircraft on the ground. Reluctantly we had to go back to school. After school we went to the site again. The RAF salvage crew had erected a temporary fence around the wreckage to keep out sight-seers. A few weeks after this the village cricket team had a fixture with a team of airmen at RAF Wittering, I cycled there with other supporters. The cricket pitch was on the landing ground near the hangers.

While the cricket match was going on an aircraft landed and taxied onto the concrete apron in front of the hangars to be refuelled. This was much more interesting than the cricket match, I went to look at the aeroplane. It was a Fairey 'Firefly', a single seater, single engine biplane fighter. While I watched the pilot reappeared wearing his leather coat and leather flying helmet and climbed into the open cockpit. The mechanics brought up a device known as a 'Huck's starter'. The engine of the 'Firefly' (from memory) was a Napier 'Lion', about five hundred horse-power, too big for easily starting by hand. The 'Huck's starter' was engaged in the propeller hub and the aircraft engine roared into life.

To me the pilot was like a god from another planet. The 'Firefly' taxied out and took off, watched until it disappeared as a speck in the distance. Fairey's used the name 'Firefly' again for a monoplane they made for the Royal Navy in about 1945. The bi-plane fighter of the late 1920's did not go into production.

The 'Hucks starter' was a device mounted on a Ford model 'T' motor car chassis to enable the power of the Ford engine to start an aero engine. On two occasions in the 1930's flying displays came to Stamford. As a landing ground they used a field about a mile to the west of the then town centre on the Empingham Road A606. The field is now built over, one of the buildings being the pub named 'The Danish Invader'. These 'Flying circuses' were organised by well known airmen of the day, one being C.W.A. Scott, the other Sir Alan Cobham. They brought a variety of aircraft for display including gliders (which were towed up by powered aircraft) and autogiro's.

At the last of these displays in 1937 they brought and demonstrated a modern single engine single seat biplane fighter built by Fairey's with the type name of 'Fantome'. It had I suspect a Rolls Royce 'Kestrel' engine which would be over six hundred horse power. They claimed it was faster than anything then in service with the RAF. It gave a great display diving and roaring low over the spectators at something like two hundred and fifty miles an hour.

In the spring of 1936 I enlisted, with friends, in the local company of the TA, Lincolnshire Regiment. This was an interesting time. We did square bashing in the Drill Hall wearing 'ammo' boots. Also in the Drill Hall we had a twenty five yard firing range and here we fired the point two-two rifles. These rifles were Lee-Enfield's as were currently in service with a bore of point three-0-three inches. Externally the .22 was exactly the same as the .303, only the bore was different.

We fired the .303 rifles on the butts at Tinwell (see map 1) at ranges of from 100 yards to 600 yards. On the same butts we fired the Lewis gun. On Sunday mornings we would clatter onto the bus hired from the local bus company and be transported up to the old aerodrome at Easton-on-the-Hill where we did exercises on the old landing ground and the surrounding fields. I say we clattered onto the bus because of the noise we made; metal studded ammo boots on the metal steps of the bus and rifles clanking against the metal frames of the seats as we 'passed right down the car'. In August we would spend two weeks under canvas. At these camps the whole of the fourth battalion would come together. 'A' company and Headquarters Company coming from Lincoln, including the band. 'B' and 'C' company came from other local towns, say Grantham, Boston and Spalding. 'D' company of course from Stamford.

The strength of each company would be over one hundred men, the battalion would be perhaps six hundred men. At the camp we would be joined by battalions of Notts and Derby's and Leicester's making up a division of about two and a half thousand men.

In the Spring/early Summer of each year the company would all come together at the 'Stamford Hotel' for the annual dinner. Dinner would be served at 8 o'clock and would be attended by all ranks wearing field service dress, including the officers. After dinner speeches would be made and toasts drunk. One of these toasts proposed by Major Jones was 'to fallen comrades'. This meant little to us teenagers but meant a lot to those who had served in WW1. We were to come to know the feelings evoked by this toast after our experiences in WW2. This practice of the officers dining once a year with the other ranks was unique to the TA of the day.

During WW1 the soldiers when marching played mouth organs and sang marching songs, this carried on in the TA between the wars. When we had the band, the band would play the most popular dance tunes of the day as marches.

At the annual camp, during the first week, we had 'adjutants parade' at about 7.15 in the morning. We would be up soon after 6 o'clock, buttons and boots polished and faces washed then to the cookhouse for 'gunfire'. 'Gunfire' consisted of a mug of boiling tea and three or four plain biscuits. Then on parade with clean rifles for inspection. As the inspecting office walked along the ranks the band would play suitable music. The bandsmen who played this music were always referred to as 'snake charmers'.

This was followed by about half an hour of drill. After 'adjutants parade' we were dismissed to the 'cookhouse' again for breakfast then about 9 o'clock 'fall in' for the serious business of the day.

On the Wednesday afternoon of the second week the battalion sports were organised. As I did well in the running on sports day Major Jones appointed me 'company runner'. During exercises I remained at Company HQ and carried written messages between the company commander and the variously deployed platoons. This appointment made life more interesting. When carrying messages the runner took action to avoid being seen by either friend or foe. This would entail running along close to hedgerows, not across open fields. Any trees, embankments, hollows etc were used to give cover.

On Coronation Day, May 12th 1937, 'D' Company fell in at the Drill Hall at about 11.30am. Each soldier was issued with three blank cartridges to suit the .303 Lee Enfield rifles. The company then marched, with Major Jones at its head, from the Drill Hall to the vicinity of the War Memorial in Broad Street. There we formed into two ranks facing towards the War Memorial.

For some weeks previously we had been practising the firing of a 'feu de joi' (fu de zhwa), now was the time for the real thing. So the rifles were loaded, pointed skywards and the fire rippled along the front rank from right to left then back along the rear rank from left to right. When the rifle bolts were opened the spent cartridge cases were ejected, about a hundred spent cartridge cases rained down with a metallic tinkle onto the hard road.

From nowhere and unexpectedly a swarm of boys appeared, aged from say eight to twelve years, on their hands and knees picking up the spent cartridge cases from around our feet. This firing procedure was repeated three times before we marched back to the Drill Hall to be dismissed. In Stamford now there is probably a seventy year old grandad showing a .303 cartridge case to his grandson and telling how he scrambled for it on the day of George VI's coronation.

These were the days of the record breaking airmen whose exploits were reported in detail in the daily press and on the BBC, as were the RAF displays at Hendon and the opening to the public of RAF stations on 'Empire Air Day' in May each year.

The newspapers were also reporting the activities of the German and Italian air forces and the outrages being perpetrated by them in Spain*. The RAF were running recruiting advertisements in the press. In response to these advertisements about the end of 1938 I filled in an application form to enlist in the RAF as an Air Observer.

* The Spanish Civil War 1936-39.

Hucks starter of the Shuttleworth Collection at Old Warden aerodrome September 1998.

Photo courtesy J. M. Harbord.

See also pages 14 and 15.

CHAPTER TWO

SYWELL

AIR OBSERVER TRAINING
JULY - OCTOBER 1939

List of illustrations etc. at the beginning of chapter 2.

Charley Wynn and Frank Harbord
Avro "Anson" aircraft

Charley Wynn   Frank Harbord

Two under-training Air-Observers at Sywell in August 1939. Charley is wearing a 'Goonskin' type parachute harness, both are wearing R.A.F. issue flying boots of the type in vogue at the time. Note all the glass around the mess entrance has been painted matt black.

Avro 'Anson' as used at No. 6 E. & R.F.T.S. at Sywell in 1939. Note the spacious 'green-house' cabin, with space for navigators chart table behind the pilot and the wireless operators station below the direction finding loop aerial.

A Vickers G. O. gun is mounted in the manually operated turret. The Armstrong-Siddeley 'Cheetah' engines of about 350 horse power each were started by a hand cranking handle. Photo coutesy - M.A.P., Aslackby, Sleaford NG34 0HG.

In February 1939 the Air Ministry summoned me to London for an interview with the RAF. After the interview and the medical examination they told me to carry on working as normal and that they would contact me in due course. About the middle of June 1939 I received a letter from the Air Ministry telling me that accommodation had been arranged for me at 130, Abington Avenue, Northampton. 'Number 6 Elementary and Reserve Flying Training School' had taken over part of St Georges College in St Georges Avenue, Northampton, and I was to report there during the morning of July 10th 1939.

So on that date about nine o'clock in the morning the train took me, with my suitcase and my bike, from the Midland station at Stamford to Northampton. The town of Northampton at that time had a population of about 105,000 and was noted for the manufacture of leather footwear and footwear making machinery. Northamptonshire County Cricket Club was always well placed in the county cricket championships and provided a number of players for the England national side. At Northampton Castle Station I put my bike into temporary storage at the station, boarded a double decker bus to St Georges College and reported as required.

130, Abington Avenue turned out to be a moderate sized house in a red brick terrace built about the turn of the century. It had three floors, five large bedrooms and was situated near the County Cricket Ground. The landlady was a widow, a Mrs Nichols, she made a living by letting the bedrooms and looking after her lodgers. One of the bedrooms I was to share with another under training Air Observer named Charley Wynn. For providing each U/T airman with board and lodgings the landlady received six shillings a day. We had no complaints about the standard of accommodation or the food. My bike was now stored in the garden shed and at the weekends I would cycle home to Stamford.

Every week day morning Charley Wynn and myself would walk along Abington Avenue to the junction with the Kettering Road (A43), cross over onto the racecourse (now a recreation ground), walk across the racecourse such that we arrived at St Georges College before nine o'clock for lectures. The distance from 130 Abington Avenue to St

Georges College was about a mile, about a twenty minute walk. The lecturers were Merchant Navy navigation officers. The principal, whose name was Isaacson, was always known as Captain Isaacson; the title 'Captain' I presumed was his Merchant Navy rank.

On the first morning we were issued with items of navigation equipment which we were to look after and bring along with us every day to lectures. These items included a course and speed calculator (CSC), pair of dividers, parallel rule, Douglas-protractor, a copy of the Air Ministry Navigation Manual (AP1234) etc.

For practical flying experience we were transported to the aerodrome at Sywell, about 6 miles north east of Northampton. The aircraft at Sywell were operated by the civil firm of Brooklands Aviation Ltd. They had there about a dozen 'Tiger Moths' for pilot training and a half a dozen 'Ansons' for observer training. The Ansons were flown by civilian pilots and usually a civilian wireless operator was carried. Two U/T observers were carried in each Anson on the exercises. Myself and Charley Wynn always flew together with a pilot named Bill Haywood. The pilots had a great age and experience advantage over the U/T observers.

The undercarriage of the Anson was retracted and lowered by muscle power. Projecting on the right hand side of the pilots seat and just below the cushion on which he sat was a spindle with a cranking handle, the throw of the crank being above five inches. As soon as the aircraft became airborne the crew began to crank up the undercarriage. The pilot could turn this crank with his right hand whilst keeping the aircraft on course with his left hand. All crew members shared in this activity, from memory it needed over a hundred revolutions of the cranking handle to fully retract the undercarriage.

Perhaps because of the undercarriage mechanism the pilot on an Anson could not use the usual pilots seat type parachute, he wore the same type of harness as other crew members. Storage was provided for the canopy packs where they were retained by bungee rubber cord. Conversation between crew members was by shouting above the engine noise. When the exercise involved vertical photography one observer would go down into the nose of the aircraft to guide the pilot over the 'target'. Alterations to the course being steered were passed from the observer in the nose to the pilot by speaking tubes, known in the RAF as 'Gosport tubes'. It took some practice before the distorted speech could be understood.

On flying days about a dozen U/T observers would be transported from St Georges College to Sywell by RAF transports. These transports, known as tenders, were small lorries of about a ton and a half capacity made by the firm of Crossley in Manchester. Similar vehicles were used in 1918 by the Royal Flying Corps and were always known as Crossley tenders. The cargo carrying area of the lorry was covered by a canvas canopy supported on a tubular steel framework.

The passengers would climb up over the tailboard and stand holding onto the canopy support frame. As soon as the tender began to move the passengers would begin to sing. A highlight of a flying day would be lunch in the mess at Sywell, always a first class affair.

Things became more serious after September 3rd 1939, following the declaration of war, but our training carried on as before. Now on our daily walks down Abington Avenue and across the racecourse we were required to carry our service respirators. We saw the branded petrol pumps in front of the garage in Abington Avenue change over to the universal single grade of 'Pool'. The red, amber and green lenses on the traffic lights were blacked out, a small cross in the centre of the lens was left clear such that the colour could be seen. The horizontal element of the cross was about three and a half inches long and half an inch wide, the vertical element being of similar dimensions.

Several times we were detailed for night flying but this was always cancelled at the last moment. Bad weather was the usual reason given. If the sky was clear then 'electrical storms' were forecast. It was about this time we first heard the saying 'only birds and fools fly, and birds don't fly at night'. The gleaming white buildings at Sywell that we could see twenty miles away from three thousand feet were now painted dark green and brown matt camouflage. Large areas of glass were painted matt black.

The navigation training course lasted three months. We spent much time plotting on Admiralty charts, Mercator's projection. For flying we used Ordnance-Survey maps, four miles to the inch, or ten miles to the inch. Time was spent on photography, meteorology, mathematics, morse code buzzer, radio direction finding and other relevant subjects. At the mid-term exam two chaps were discharged due to air sickness and three others who failed to reach the required standard were discharged.

At the end of the course, after the final exams, a Royal Air Force Officer in the uniform of a Squadron Leader turned up at St. Georges College for the purpose of 'swearing in' the remaining fifty five or so successful candidates. At this 'swearing in' each candidate was given a unique service number; these numbers ranged from approx. 581195 to 581255, my number was 581215.

We were the last course of air observers to be trained at Sywell.

CHAPTER THREE

ALDERGROVE

BOMBING AND GUNNERY SCHOOL
OCTOBER & NOVEMBER 1939

FOR LOCATION OF PLACES REFERREDTO IN THIS CHAPTER SEE MAP 2

List of illustrations etc. at the beginning of chapter 3.

Map No. 2
53 Squadron Blenheim
Layout and explanation of Bombing Range
Handley Page "Heyford"
Hawker "Henley"
Westland "Wapiti"
Fairey "Battle"
Signatures, course photograph and names at Aldergrove, 1939.

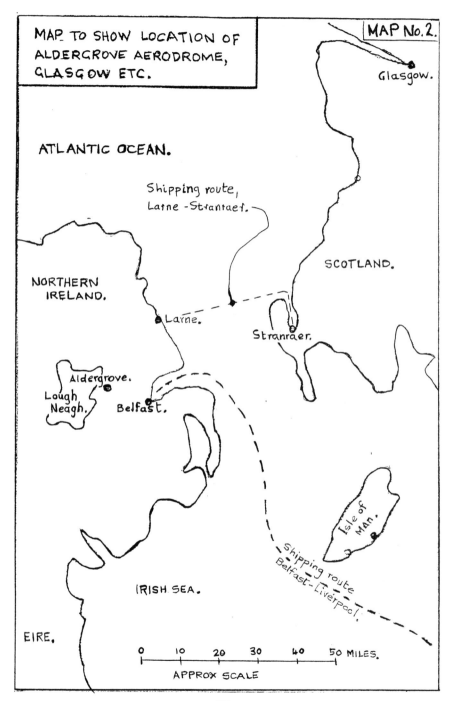

MAP TO SHOW LOCATION OF
ALDERGROVE AERODROME,
GLASGOW ETC.

MAP No. 2.

Glasgow.

ATLANTIC OCEAN.

Shipping route,
Larne - Stranraer.

SCOTLAND.

NORTHERN
IRELAND.

Larne.

Stranraer.

Aldergrove.

Lough
Neagh.

Belfast.

Isle of
Man.

IRISH SEA.

Shipping route
Belfast - Liverpool.

EIRE.

0   10   20   30   40   50 MILES.
APPROX SCALE

Four local beauties pose on the wreckage of the 53 Squadron Mk.IV
Blenheim PZ–W in the summer of 1940. See text at end of chapter 3.
Photograph coutesty S/L Don McLeod R.A.F. (Ret'd.)

TYPICAL LAYOUT OF
R.A.F. PRACTICE BOMBING RANGE

The target to be aimed at was set up in the water a thousand to fifteen hundred yards from the land. The range control tower, with its signals area, and the two observation towers were set up on the land as shown in the diagram on page 41.

It was all so arranged that the lines of bearing from the observation towers to the target formed an approximate right angle where they crossed over the target.

Before dropping any bombs, an aircraft's crew would examine the signals area in front of the range control tower. If all was clear to start bombing two white discs about eight feet in diameter would be displayed in the signals area and the bombing programme could commence.

If only one disc was displayed this told the pilot not to bomb, but to await further instructions.

If a second disc was added bombing could commence. If the one original disc was covered such that no discs were visible, the pilot must return to base as the range was closed.

As well as the 'line of bearing', each observation tower would record the precise time of each bomb and the heading of the aircraft.

After the bombing programme was completed the lines of bearing for each bomb would be laid off on an accurately printed to scale map of the range.

Where the lines of bearing crossed was the position of that bomb. A separate map of the range was used for each bomb.

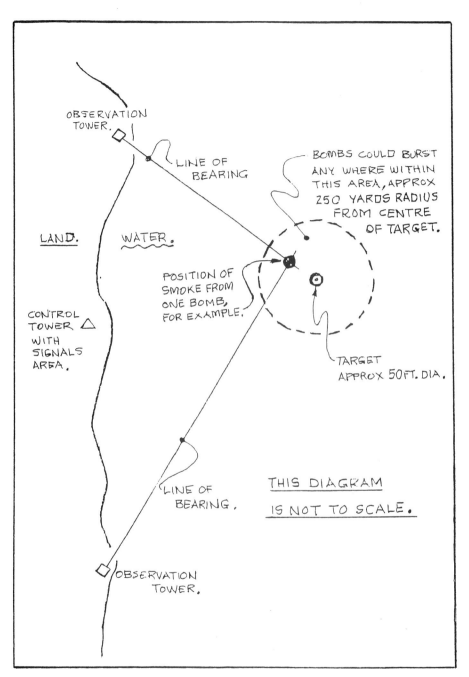

Diagram to show typical layout of practice bombing range.

The above photograph shows a side view of a Handley Page Ltd. "Heyford" bomber as used for practice bombing at Aldergrove in 1939. Note Lewis gun in the nose turret and the mid-upper turret. A Lewis gun was also fitted in the ventral turret which is shown in this photograph, when not in use this 'dustbin' could be retracted into the aircraft's fuselage. This ventral turret was the forerunner of the ventral ball turret used on the U.S.A.A.F. B17s during World War Two.

Photo coutesy - M.A.P., Aslackby, Sleaford NG34 0MG

Hawker "Henley" of the type used for drogue towing at Aldergrove in 1939
Photo courtesy M.A.P., Aslackby, Sleaford NG34 0HG

Westland Ltd. "Wapiti" as used for air firing practice at Aldergrove in 1939. Note the Lewis gun on the "Scarff" ring around the rear cockpit.
Photo courtesy M.A.P., Aslackby, Sleaford NG34 0HG

The above photograph shows the Fairey "Battle" as used for air firing practice at Aldergrove in 1939. Similar aircraft were based at West Raynham and used for drogue towing over the firing range at Wainfleet Sands in the spring and summer of 1940. It was on this type of aircraft that Flying Officer Garland and Sgt. Gray of No. 12 Squadron R.A.F. won their V.C.s in May 1940.
Reproduced with kind permission of Comm. Squadron Aviation Photos.

BOMBING and GUNNERY COURSE, ALDERGROVE, October 1939

BOMBING and GUNNERY COURSE, ALDERGROVE, October 1939

Back row, standing, from left to right:

1 & 2 unknown; 3 A.N. Holmes; 4 unknown; 5 G. Cook; 6 J. Davis; 7 unknown; 8 Langford; 9 unknown; 10 W. Brooks; 11 Craven; 12 J. Archer-Crump; 13 unknown; 14 Hicks; 15 unknown; 16 Holland; 17 F Harbord.

Front row, sitting, from left to right:

18 unknown; 19 J. Friendly; 20 Douglas-Brown; 21 Griffin; 22 C. Hamilton; 23 R Collinge; 24 Gibson; 25 L.S. Coleman; 26 R. Harding; 27 Adlam; 28 unknown; 29 Tim Howe; 30 unknown.

Some of the chaps in the photograph signed on the back of the print, these signatures are reproduced on page 48.

R. Hilton

A. N. Holmes.

Leonard S. Colman.

E. Branks..

J. Cook (Cookie)

R. H. Holland

R. Gibson (Gibby)

Wilfred J. Stafford.

J. R. Davis (Red).

C. Howe

Reg. Harding

J. Dougls. Brown.

R. T. Griffin

J. Cornish

W. E. Hood

BOMBING & GUNNERY
COURSE
ALDERGROVE IRELAND
NOVEMBER 1939

I am on the extreme
right.

The signatures reproduced above were written
on the back of a print of the photograph on page 46.

In mid October 1939 the navigation course at Northampton/ Sywell came to an end. The fifty five chaps were split into two groups of approximately equal size. It seemed that whoever made the arrangements took the list of names in alphabetical order and put the first A to Aldergrove, the second to Porthcawl the third to Aldergrove and so on; or it may have been just a random selection. My name was on the list to go to Aldergrove in Northern Ireland. Porthcawl is in south Wales. I didn't know it at the time but this was the first of many strokes of good luck that I was to benefit from all through the war.

The group that went to Porthcawl then went on to Andover then on to the Battle and Blenheim squadrons in France where they were massacred in May and June 1940. The Aldergrove group went afterwards to units based in the UK where they were cushioned from the extreme violence of the 1940 Battle of France.

The Aldergrove group left Northampton by train on a Saturday morning in mid October 1939 and travelled to Liverpool. Due to changing trains and long waits at various junctions it was dark by the time we arrived at Liverpool. By the time we sailed in the 'Ulster Queen', the ferry to Belfast, it must have been midnight. We arrived on the dockside at Belfast about half past seven on a cold misty October Sunday morning.

After a wait of an hour or two, transport came from the camp at Aldergrove to pick us up. At the camp we were met by the Station Warrant Officer (SWO) who escorted us to the Airmen's mess and ordered breakfast for us. We were all dressed in civilian clothes but were rated as leading aircraftmen (LAC's). During our first week at Aldergrove we were 'kitted out' from the station stores.

At Aldergrove we did practice bombing on Heyford's, dropping bombs - practice, smoke, eleven and a half pounds. We learned practice bombs were always painted grey. Explosive bombs were painted a service yellow. The lecturers were mostly Flight Sergeants with many years of service, one was a Warrant Officer. We dropped the bombs from an altitude of six thousand feet onto targets set up in Lough Neagh.

In the lecture rooms we studied the theory of the bomb sight and the trajectory of various bombs. This involved some trigonometry ; Claude Hamilton would always question the theory and the trigonometry and earned himself the nickname of the 'cosine king'. We learned about the Lewis gun, stripping cleaning and reassembling, also the naming of parts. Likewise the Vickers GO gun and the Browning. We fired the Lewis at ground targets from Wapiti's. Before flying we filled the Lewis drum with ninety eight rounds of .303 ammunition, and took the full drum with us. After firing we took the empty or partially used drum back to the armoury.

The programme for these firing flights was very detailed, and the times had to be maintained. If it was an afternoon the first observer was up at 14.00 hours. The pilot had to be there in the aircraft with his engine running ready for take off at 14.00 hours. He had to taxi out, take off, climb, fly to the targets, fly up and down over the targets while the observer fired the gun then fly back to the aerodrome, land and taxi in, change observers, and be ready for take off again at, say, 14.30 hours.

The observer had to be in the crew room dressed ready for flying and clutching his drum of ammunition a quarter of an hour before the time of take-off. A sergeant ACH, GD, was appointed to make sure the pilot was not kept waiting for his observer. This sergeant was always hovering about just outside the crew room door in an agitated state. He had the detailed programme on his clip board and when he saw a U/T observer approaching from about fifty yards away he would call out 'come on, hurry up, you're late, what's your name?'

On the Wapiti the gun was mounted on a 'Scarff ring', a parachute was stowed in the cockpit. As a safeguard against falling out we always engaged the 'monkey buckle'. This quick release buckle was affixed to a very strong webbing strap which in turn was attached very securely to the aircraft structure. The quick release buckle was engaged to a metal ring affixed to the bottom end of the parachute harness and at the back such that if the aircraft turned over the observer would be retained to the aircraft like a monkey hanging by its tail.

We fired the Vickers GO gun from Fairey 'Battles' at drogue's towed by Hawker 'Henley's'. We filled the hundred round drums in the armoury. On the Lewis gun the drum was rotated by a ratchet mechanism to feed the rounds to the gun. On the GO gun the drum did not rotate, the rounds were pushed around inside the drum by a spring to feed the gun.

To be able to load the rounds into the GO gun drum the spring tension had to be released. When the drum was full the tension on the feed spring had to be restored. Devices for releasing and restoring the tension on the feed spring were fixed to the work benches in the armoury. These devices were hand operated.

Two observers would fly in the same 'Battle' and fire at the same drogue. In order to be able to know how many hits on the drogue were scored by each observer one of the observers would fill his drum with red tipped rounds. The red tipped rounds were ordinary rounds the noses of which had been dipped into red paint. They would leave a hole in the drogue with a red edge. While one observer was firing from the air gunners station the other one would wait in the navigators station. Changing over positions, wearing flying clothing, parachute harness etc was difficult.

To be able to credit the hits on the drogue to the correct observer timing was important. It was recorded at what time a drogue was streamed and dropped. It was known who was up in the Battle at that time and which observer was firing red and which plain.

As well as firing real guns in the air we fired the camera gun from the ground. The camera gun was really a camera dressed up to look like an aircraft machine gun. It was fitted with the normal 'ring and bead' sight. The camera gun was fitted onto a 'Scarff' ring which in turn was fitted to a framework firmly fixed to the ground.

A 'Gladiator' would make simulated attacks on the camera gun station and would fly past at various distances, altitudes and speeds. The gunner would aim the gun at the aircraft making the proper allowances for speed & range. When the gun was fired the camera would take a photograph of the aircraft. These photographs would be examined by the instructors who would assess the deflection allowances made by the gunner.

The building we lived in at Aldergrove was known as the

'hostel'. After lectures or flying or whatever was on the go, at about 16.30 hours we would fall in on the parade ground for a half an hours drill by the station warrant officer.

At the end of the course we had a written exam on the theory and a practical/oral exam, dismantling or assembling the Lewis or Vickers GO gun, naming the parts and cleaning them with oil, anti-freeze. They were great days, full of interest.

When the course was finished we were split up into parties of about six chaps to each party, and each party posted to a different RAF station in the UK. I was in the party posted to Bicester in Oxfordshire. Late on a Saturday afternoon in late November 1939 we were taken by motor transport to Larne about thirty five miles north of Belfast. At Larne we boarded the ferry for Stranraer (in Scotland, Wigtown).

Somehow we caught a through train to London, travelling overnight. After various delays we caught another train back up to Bletchley where after further delays we caught a train for Bicester. In those days as I remember the trains were warm and comfortable as were the waiting rooms on the stations. The refreshment rooms on the stations were comfortable and provided reasonable food.

The following account of the loss of Blenheim No L4860 (PZ-W) of 53 Squadron is typical of the kind of thing that happened to the chaps on the course at Sywell who went to Porthcawl when I went to Aldergrove.

THE END OF BLENHEIM (MARK IV)
No L 4860 PZ. W of 53 SQUADRON

On the 15th May 1940 a Blenheim of 53 Squadron took off from Poix de Picardie to fly to the advanced aerodrome at Vitry-en-Artois. This aircraft belonged to the AASF (Advanced Air Strike Force) and 53 Squadron was part of the Air Support Command to the army in France.

On the 16th May the crew of this aircraft: Pilot, P/O Lovell, Observer Sgt McLeod and W. Op/AG Kenneth were briefed by an army major at 4 o'clock in the morning. They were to patrol for two hours along part of the Albert Canal and report on troop movement. The instructions they were given were not at all clear. The army major had little idea of the position of the advancing German army. He advised that the aircraft should be flown at 3,700 feet. At that height he said the aircraft would be too high for the small arms fire and too low to be worried by heavy flak. No mention was made of enemy fighters.

Just before 4.30am the aircraft took off and rendezvoused with two Hurricane escort fighters. There was no inter-communication between the Blenheim and the Hurricane escort. At about 5am the aircraft was over the target and encountered the usual flak. Suddenly this ceased and directly out of the glare of the morning sun a formation of ME 109s swooped down on the Blenheim. Immediately the Hurricane escort left the formation and presumably attacked the German fighters, leaving the Blenheim without protection. The Blenheim was then attacked by a number of German fighters in line astern, one following the other. The air gunner valiantly fired his Vickers GO armed with 303 bullets. The German fighters stood off at 1,000 yards and if the 303s reached the fighters they could have done little damage at that range. The ME 109s fired explosive canon shells into the Blenheim and the three occupants were severely wounded. With a superb effort the pilot, although wounded, crashed the aircraft into a ploughed field, wheels up.

Fortunately the aircraft did not catch fire and the observer and air gunner managed to get the pilot out of the damaged aircraft and after giving him a morphine injection waited in a dazed condition for help to arrive. The observer received shrapnel wounds in the back of his head, in the back and through the leg. The pilot was shot through the legs and up through the chin. The AG seemed to be the least wounded.

At about 5.15am two women came and helped the crew. One woman went to her cottage nearby to fetch a pillow to support the pilot's head. The navigator's head was bandaged to stop the flow of blood. Eventually the crew were taken in a truck to a clinic where their wounds were dressed.

The pilot and observer were separated but both eventually reached England.

The observer found himself, as the only English man in a French hotel (the Grand Hotel at Deauville) which was being used as a casualty clearing station for the wounded French soldiers. He had the shrapnel removed from his head by a French army surgeon.

As the Germans advanced the 'hospital' was to be evacuated to Bordeau. By chance a British army lorry was passing and the observer was taken by the two British soldiers, who were themselves trying to reach the coast. They stayed one night a Caen before reaching the coast at Cherbourg being taken on the last boat to England. The observer owes his life to the tender care given to him by these two soldiers.

In the confusion of the retreat contact was lost with the W.Op. Leading Aircraftman A.G. Kenneth, examination of records show him listed as missing.

Above report courtesy of S/L Don McLeod RAF (Ret'd)

CHAPTER FOUR

BICESTER, FOR THE FIRST TIME, NOVEMBER 1939 - MARCH 1940

104 SQUADRON
FOR LOCATION OF PLACES REFERRED
TO IN THIS CHAPTER SEE MAP 3

List of illustrations etc. at the beginning of chapter 4

Map No. 3.
Bicester Market Square.
Photo of Frank Harbord in the barrack hut at Bicester, December 1939 and caption.

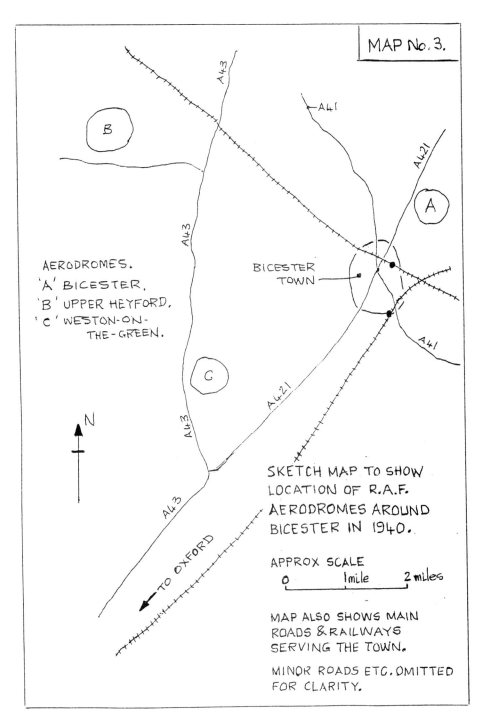

MAP No. 3.

B

A43

A41

A421

A

AERODROMES.
'A' BICESTER,
'B' UPPER HEYFORD,
'C' WESTON-ON-
      THE-GREEN.

BICESTER
TOWN

A43

A41

C

A421

N

A43

TO OXFORD

SKETCH MAP TO SHOW
LOCATION OF R.A.F.
AERODROMES AROUND
BICESTER IN 1940.

APPROX SCALE
0   1mile   2 miles

MAP ALSO SHOWS MAIN
ROADS & RAILWAYS
SERVING THE TOWN.

MINOR ROADS ETC. OMITTED
FOR CLARITY.

Bicester Market Square / Sheep Street as it was in 1939.

Frank Harbord in the barrack hut at Bicester in December 1939

Caption to photograph on page 58.

Frank Harbord in the barrack hut at Bicester in December 1939

The bedding is stacked in the approved manner, three "biscuits", (these were laid out at night to form a mattress), pillow and sheets wrapped in blankets on the top.

In the middle of the hut is the "Tortoise" slow combustion coke burning stove with its chimney pipe going up out of the roof. The stove is mounted on a concrete base. Coke is stored in the rectangular metal container at the side of the stove.

The hut was of timber construction, the wooden floor being covered with the usual brown polished linoleum. The interior of the hut was illuminated by two sixty watt electric bulbs, any higher rated lamps were confiscated on the daily inspection.

The photograph was posed for as I was going out, note I am properly dressed with my respirator strap over my right shoulder and gleaming overcoat buttons. The photograph was taken using a box camera in natural daylight.

We arrived at the LMS railway station at Bicester on a murky Sunday afternoon about 2pm. A taxi took us up to the gates of the camp.

We were all acting Sergeants, Acting Air Observers on probation, but wore no stripes or brevet's. We were not allowed to wear the air observers brevet until we had completed our six months probation. The authorities at Aldergrove had given us the stripes, we were instructed to sew them on while in transit. Suitable needles, thread, thimble etc was contained in the 'housewife', which was issued to each of us. This task was found to be not so easy as it at first sounds and it was not completed until we were at Bicester. One of our number (named Adlam) had done some tailoring work before joining the RAF. He found from somewhere sufficient dressmakers pins so that we could pin the stripes in position while we did the sewing. Using the pins the task became possible, we found it virtually impossible without the aid of the pins.

Bicester aerodrome is situated about two and a half miles north-north-east of the market place in the old town. The landing field, a large grass field, is on the east side of the old Roman road now known as the A421.

Between the road (A421) and the four large aircraft hangars are all the technical buildings. Just inside the entrance gates is the guard-room and Station Headquarters. The living accommodation, the various messes and all domestic buildings are on the west side of the A421.

After the taxi dropped us outside the entrance gates it was to the guard room that we reported. We were soon taken in charge by a Flight Sergeant Devlin. The Flight Sergeant was grey haired, obviously a reservist recalled when the war had broken out. On this Sunday he was orderly sergeant. We were reassured by his air of efficiency and authority and by his smart appearance, particularly the glittering buttons on his coat and the similarly glittering crowns above his sergeant's stripes indicating his rank.

Carrying our kitbags we all followed F/S Devlin out of the main gates across the road and into the domestic camp. A hut was found where there were sufficient vacant beds to accommodate us all. He gave some instructions regarding the mess and told us to report to the orderly room in Station HQ in the morning.

In the orderly room on the Monday morning we discovered that two squadrons of Blenheim's were based at Bicester, no's 104 and 108. Each squadron was divided into two flights, 'A' and 'B'. Each of the four hangars was occupied by one flight. Following the usual RAF procedure the five of us were split up between the squadrons and the flights, I was to report to 'B' flight of 104 squadron.

During our short experience we had been given no instruction as to the function and duties of various people on the Squadrons. We now found out the squadron had a flight -sergeant discip. In this instance his name was Newton. The squadron was organised as a training squadron, having a permanent core of experienced pilots, observers and wireless operator/air gunners. These accounted for about a quarter of the strength of the flight. The flight had, say, ten Blenheim's, a mixture of MK1's and Mk IV's and perhaps three Anson's. At that stage of the war (December '39) all these aircraft would be carefully pushed into the hangar before 5 o'clock in the afternoon and the hangar doors closed. When night flying was on the programme the required aircraft would be parked on the apron outside the hanger.

The CO of 104 Squadron was W/C Coggle, I never did get to see him. He was a mysterious figure that was spoken about and whose signature appeared in flying log books at the end of each month. The Flight Commander was S/L Arnold Christian (a relative, it was said, of Fletcher Christian of 'Mutiny on the Bounty' fame). About the same date that our small party from Aldergrove joined 104 other observers at a similar stage of training joined the squadron from other observer training schools, such as Prestwick (Scotland), Jurby on the Isle of Man and Ansty near Coventry.

On the strength of the flight then we had about a half dozen air observers under training plus three or four very experienced observers about 30 years old, very weather beaten and grizzled. These chaps would have been in the RAF some years, most likely they would have joined as apprentices and trained at Halton.

61

As pilots on the flight we had S/L Christian, a couple of F/Ls, both had the same surname of Thomas but were very different characters, one was a reserved quiet English gentleman the other a noisy brash Australian with a handle-bar moustache. Another pilot was a Canadian F/O named Bauld, another F/O named Starr who was ex Imperial Airways and the navigation expert on the flight.

Those listed in the above paragraph were considered 'staff' pilots. The S/L had his office, the other staff pilots had their own 'den' next to the S/L's office where they would congregate and do whatever they did when they were not flying.

As well as the staff pilots we had a couple of sergeant pilots who had come up through long service in the ranks, a couple of Auxiliary Air Force Sergeant Pilots under training and two or three young Pilot Officers still under training.

On that first Monday I, with others, did get to meet S/L Christian. He told us he was the Flight Commander and that he gave the orders and nobody else. To me at the time he appeared to be more like Captain Bligh than Fletcher Christian. Due to the urgency of the situation we were working a seven day week and a twenty-four hour day. Each individual would have one day off in seven, staggered such that every day the bulk of the flight was available for duty.

We would all report to the crew room every morning at 08.30 hours, if not required for flying we would attend various lectures arranged by the Chief Ground Instructor. At these lectures the register would be called (as it was called in the state schools in the 1930's). Some of the names on those registers now appear on headstones in the churchyard of Caversfield Church near the aerodrome, most others will be on headstones in military cemeteries in various parts of the world.

The Blenheim needed a crew of three, pilot, observer and wireless operator/air gunner. At that time Wop/AG's were ground wireless ops who volunteered for flying duty. They would vary in rank from AC2 to LAC. They wore the 'sparks' badge of the wireless operator and the brass winged bullet badge of the air gunner. These badges were worn on the tunic sleeve.

Every morning at 08.30 the observers, sergeant pilots and U/T officer pilots would assemble in the crew room. The crew room was a large room estimated about forty feet long by fifteen feet wide built into and alongside the hanger. The main item of furniture in the crew room was a large table estimated twenty feet long by seven feet wide with a smooth green top. The large area was necessary to enable a number of observers to spread out maps or charts to work out flight plans at the same time. Also the crew room had enough chairs for all to have a seat while waiting.

In the hangar near to the flight commanders office stood a large crude wooden lectern. On this lectern rested the Flight Authorisation Book. This was a book with pages of about the present day A3 size. These pages were ruled with horizontal lines and vertical columns. The column headings calling for details such as aircraft numbers, types, pilot and crews name, details of the exercise to be carried out, time of take off etc.

The Flight Authorisation Book was of great importance. The book would disappear into the flight commanders office before 08.30 hours and would re-appear on the lectern any time up to say 12.00 hours. It was up to each individual to read the book and to be off the ground by the appointed time. It was the duty of the observer to collect a weather forecast from the met office. He also had to collect the bomb sight from the armoury and install it and make sure it was fitted with the correct height scale for the bombs (imaginary) that were being carried.

If photographs were required it was up to the observer to collect the necessary camera from the photographic section and install it in the aircraft. The earlier you saw the authorisation book the more time was available to carry out the pre-flight activities. Usually due to pressure of time only the course for the first leg of the flight was worked out in the crew room, the remainder had to be done in the air.

One of our grizzled observers, Sgt Jones, always seemed to know when the book was out. He would be apparently absorbed in a game of cards when he would walk out of the crew room down the hangar, look on the lectern and come back to announce the book was out. This would be the start of frenzied activity. Flying clothing, parachutes etc must be retrieved from flying clothing lockers, contact had to be made between pilots, observers and wireless op's. If the flight was not off the ground by the appointed time S/L Christian would want to know why.

Due to their lowly rank the W/Op's did not sit in the crew room with the SNCO's, they must have had their own den somewhere. Whatever the arrangement was they would appear at the right time and all ready for action. Once off the ground the first entry in the navigation log was 'airborne base'. No names for security reasons.

Before leaving the vicinity of the aerodrome the pilot would ask the W.Op./AG to get 'WT GO' from the ground station. This ensured the wireless was working and that no last minute hitch had arisen. When the W.Op./AG reported he had 'WT GO' this was entered in the navigation log and the first course would be set, the pilot climbing to a height as specified in the details of the exercise or to a height chosen at his discretion to suit the weather conditions and the terrain.

We wore leather flying helmets. At that time each airman would be issued with a helmet of a suitable size but minus facilities for fitting ear phones. Each airman would mark on the helmet the position of his ears such that the required hole could be cut and the necessary fittings stitched in place. On the outside of the helmet and covering these fittings was stitched a leather disc (of similar material to the helmet itself) about four inches diameter. This disc had a zip fastener running across the middle and arranged vertically such that when the slider was at the top the zip was open.

Earphones could then be clipped into the fitting with the cable hanging downwards. A moulded piece of sponge rubber was pushed into the space between the earphone and the outer zipped cover. When all was snug the zip could be pulled down to hold everything in place. About fifteen inches away from each earphone the two earphone cables merged. The thicker cable then went on about a yard long ending in a jack plug.

From the point where the earphone cables merged a third cable emerged about fifteen inches long leading to a microphone. The microphone was fitted into the nose of the oxygen mask. This mask made of soft leather fitted under the chin and covered the mouth and nose, it clipped to the helmet by four press studs. Unless oxygen was being used the mask would be left dangling from two press studs on one side of the helmet. The mask would be held over the face by hand when it was necessary to use the microphone.

All aircrew were issued with white silk gloves, woollen gloves, leather gauntlets and Sidcot suits. A Sidcot suit consisted of a warm 'inner', a waterproof 'outer' and a fur collar. Black, fleecy lined, leather, knee length flying boots. 'Irvin' flying jackets and trousers were also available. Various combinations of all the above items were worn on different occasions as suited the time of year, the altitude, and the experience and the whim of the airmen.

The pilot wore a 'seat' type parachute. The observer and W.Op./AG wore a harness with clips on the chest to accept the parachute pack, this allowed them to move about in the aircraft. The 'inter comm' and oxygen could be plugged in at convenient points. Stowage points for the parachute packs were provided in the aircraft.

The cameras used at that time were Williamson Eagle's, F24's, and could be fitted with lenses of various focal lengths. The negative size was five inches square. I still remember the formula $W/F = L/H$, where W = length of side of negative (always five inches with the F24 camera) F = focal length of lens in inches, L = length of ground in feet covered by the negative and H = height (altitude). This was remembered as Whilst Looking For Height.

Altitude was always measured in feet. Various sized magazines could be fitted to the camera, some of them containing enough film for over a hundred exposures. Knowing the length of ground covered by the negative and the ground speed of the aircraft a suitable time interval could be selected between each exposure such that a desired overlap was obtained. Before taking any photographs the W.OP./AG was required to level the camera by means of the 'fore and aft' and 'transverse' spirit levels and to set the 'drift' on the scale provided. The 'drift', which was always being checked by the observer, was passed to the W.Op/AG over the intercom. The camera was mounted in the fuselage about level with the trailing edge of the wing so was only accessible to the W.Op/AG. The operation of the camera was controlled by the observer in the nose of the aircraft by means of electrical switches.

Some flights made from Bicester while I was acting air observer on probation stand out in my memory. One was a flight in a 'vee' formation of five aircraft led by S/L Christian (all Mk IV Blenheims) who my pilot was that day or our position in the formation I cannot recollect. We probably flew at an altitude of three to four thousand feet, to Exeter. We circled over Exeter and descended to about eight hundred feet and made two ro three circuits around the cathedral before setting off back to Bicester.

A Royal Air Force officer known to S/L Christian was married in the cathedral that day and the idea was that the squadron should be overhead when they came out of the cathedral. I knew nothing then of the beauty of the building or its stained glass windows and never dreamed that it would suffer bomb damage during the war.

One of our exercises was to fly down to Lyme Bay and at a position a few miles out to sea from Sidmouth to drop a sea marker. The sea marker was a streamlined aluminium cannister about five inches diameter by a foot long with stabilizing fins. It would be carried on the flare racks either under the fuselage or under one of the wings. The casing of the sea marker was of thin aluminium, the interior was packed with aluminium powder ground very fine to be almost like flour. It was all arranged such that on impact with the sea the casing burst and the aluminium powder spread on the water to give a disc of aluminium colour about thirty feet in diameter.

The aluminium disc was then used as a target for practice bombing. We would approach the target from four different directions and on each run would drop a practice (smoke) bomb weighing eleven and a half pounds. These practice bombs would also be carried on the flare racks.

A few days after carrying out this exercise with practice bombs we were detailed to do it again but this time we would be carrying four by two hundred and fifty pound live general purpose bombs. Live bombs were painted yellow, practice bombs were painted grey. The live bombs would be instantaneously fused, to burst on impact. The minimum altitude for dropping these bombs was one thousand feet, if dropped from a lower altitude the aircraft was liable to suffer damage from blast and shrapnel.

This exercise, as well as a navigation exercise, would give the pilot experience of the feel of the aircraft with a full load and the feel as the bombs were dropped. Six thousand feet was the preferred bombing altitude. The weather forecast for the Lyme Bay area was not good. We were instructed that if the weather over Lyme Bay was not suitable to carry out the exercise we were to land at Boscombe Down where the bombs would be made safe before we flew back to Bicester.

The pilot on this occasion was a young under-training pilot officer named Gilbert. In the vicinity of Salisbury Plain the weather was deteriorating and over Lyme Bay the cloud base was about fifteen hundred feet and rain was falling. Under these conditions the exercise could not be completed. We therefore landed at Boscombe Down as instructed. We reported to the duty pilot in the watch office and asked for the bombs to be made safe. This caused much bewilderment to all concerned, Boscombe Down claimed they were not aware that crews were being instructed to land there to have bombs made safe.

After much chat and telephone conversations between the watch office and the various people on the camp and an hour or two delay a couple of armourers did come and replaced the safety pins in the bombs and disconnected the arming devices before we flew back to Bicester. We never did carry out this exercise with live bombs.

On another occasion I was doing a navigation exercise over north Wales in an Anson flown by Sergeant Whitaker. To oversee my efforts that day we had on board Sgt Jones, as well as the usual wireless operator. At one of the turning points I handed the new course to Sgt Whitaker, he set it on the compass, turned the aircraft and settled down. A couple of minutes later Sgt Jones lifted the side of Sgt Whitaker's helmet and shouted above the roar of the engines, 'you are being a silly b———!' This was a surprise to me, an under training air observer certainly would not have dreamed of talking to a pilot like that. Sgt Whitaker checked over all his instruments saw nothing wrong but was obviously puzzled. A few minutes later, with a wink to me, Sgt Jones repeated his comment into Sgt Whitaker's ear. I also could see nothing amiss. Again Sgt Whitaker checked over all his instruments and again saw nothing amiss.

After another couple of minutes the side of Sgt Whitaker helmet was lifted and Sgt Jones yelled into his ear 'wake up, wake up, look at your compass.' We could all then see that although the correct number of degrees had been set against the lubber line the south end of the compass needle was where the north end should have been, we were therefore flying a reciprocal course. Sgt Whitaker made a one hundred and eighty degree turn back to the original turning point and started again, this time making no mistake.

This incident did show the necessity for constant vigilance by all members of an aircraft's crew. Even an experienced captain of aircraft could make a mistake. The life of each member of the crew always depended on the vigilance and efficiency of all the other members.

One day in January 1940 I was detailed to fly with a Sgt Hettrick. It was to be a long range formation exercise. An officer pilot was leading, the other two aircraft making up the V were flown by Sgt Whitaker and Sgt Hettrick, our first turning point was Worcester. Over Worcester we noticed that Sgt Whitaker was missing. The formation leader turned back towards Bicester. Sgt Hettrick said to me 'we'll carry on alone', I agreed and we set course alone for the next turning point which was Rhyll. From Rhyll we went on to Jurby in the Isle of Man then to Fishguard (South Wales). From Fishguard we set course for Bicester.

After Cheltenham visibility was deteriorating and I lost track of the map reading. At ETA for Bicester we were about two thousand feet and visibility was about one mile. As the fuel gauges were showing just about empty the pilot decided to land in a grass field while he still had engines and control. This he did, we telephoned to Bicester and a tender came to pick us up. We knew we were within a few miles of Bicester although we could not see it and had asked the W. Op. to get a bearing from Bicester or anywhere else that he could raise. In the language of the day there was 'no joy' on the wireless, despite getting 'W.T. Go' after take off.

Many most valuable lessons were learned from this experience. One was never put any faith in getting navigation assistance from the wireless. We also learned about the fuel system on the MK IV Blenheim. The Mk I Blenheim had two fuel tanks situated in the wings between the fuselage and the engines. The Mk IV had two extra tanks outboard from the engines. It was considered that the wing was not strong enough to withstand landing with these outer tanks full. The outer tanks therefore were fitted with jettison pipes and on training establishments the outer tanks were not to be filled.

Both the pilot and myself were surprised that the fuel gauges for the inner tanks were showing empty when we arrived back in the vicinity of Bicester. Subsequent investigation found that fuel had seeped from the full inner tanks into the empty outer tanks, such that we still had enough fuel on board for over half an hour's flying. If we had known this fuel was available we would have had time to find Bicester aerodrome.

On the Blenheim the fuel tank contents gauge does not register until activated, one dial serves all four tanks. To get an indication of how much fuel is in a tank the pilot had first to select which tank he is interested in by rotating a knob just below the gauge dial, to one of four positions. Then when the same knob is pressed the needle on the dial shows how much fuel is in that tank as a proportion of the maximum contents. When the knob is released the gauge is deactivated and the needle returns to read zero.

We also found out that what ever happened to the rest of the formation we should have stayed with the formation leader. Back at Bicester we learned that Sgt Whitaker had left the formation and returned to Bicester because of engine failure. While landing at Bicester on one engine he had hit a tree on the aerodrome boundary. The aircraft was wrecked although the crew escaped uninjured. Subsequent investigation showed that the engine failure was caused by a failure in the fuel supply.

One of the exercises we did was a 'war load climb'. A Mk IV was loaded with four inert filled two hundred and fifty pound bombs and a full load of fuel. The pilot would take off and climb. At ten thousand feet the crew went on to oxygen, the climb continued. The oxygen supply being increased at fifteen thousand feet. At twenty thousand feet the oxygen supply increased again as the aircraft was levelled off. After about ten minutes at this altitude a descent back to the aerodrome was started. To even out the pressure in the ears pinch the nose and blow, do this when below ten thousand feet and the oxygen mask has been removed from the face.

A few days before Christmas 1939 on a murky afternoon when there was no flying at Bicester the sound of aircraft engines was heard. Six 'Battles' in formation appeared overhead, went into line astern and landed one after the other, taxied up to the hangars, parked, and shut off. The aircraft were mud bespattered. We became aware that they were part of a squadron from the Advanced Air Striking Force based in France. The squadron was flying back to the UK to dump the 'Battles' and re-equip with Blenheim's.

The squadron was not routed to Bicester; they landed there as the weather was too bad for them to go on to their original destination. These aircraft and crews were objects of much curiosity and admiration amongst the under training crews at Bicester. They had been 'over the lines', had even survived seeing Messerschmitt's. The confidence amongst the crews, the bonhomie, the panache, handlebar moustaches and issue gaiters they wore around their ankles were causes of wonder. As well as all that having come from France and as it was approaching Christmas much French hooch was stowed in each aircraft. Even more hooch suitably affixed to the bomb racks. Of the eighteen men who flew in on the six Battle's, six, say were officers, six SNCO's and six of lesser rank. The hooch would have been fairly shared out between the messes, in all the arrival of the Battle's gave rise to a very jolly evening. What the squadron number was and where they went to when they took off next day I don't now recall.

By mid January 1940, the weather turned rough, snow fell and put a stop to flying training. The authorities took the opportunity to send the U/T airmen on leave and to institute a heavy programme of lectures and ground training.

70

About this time a number, perhaps a dozen, Finnish pilots appeared in the sergeants mess. They wore civilian clothes and spoke varying amounts of English. They were at Bicester to be trained·on the Blenheim and to gain experience on the type. At the same time RAF Blenheims began to disappear into one of the hangars to emerge a few days later with the British national marking changed to the Finnish swastika. Squadron identification letters were removed and the original aircraft numbers removed and new numbers substituted using a bigger type of character. These aircraft were eventually flown to Finland and used in the war against Russia. (In June 1941 Finland allied herself to Germany).

Amongst the under training crews on 108 Squadron was a sergeant pilot always known as Jock, he was a Scot, his real name I cannot now recall. When the snow was on the ground and we were told we could go on leave he was so anxious to get to his billet to collect his luggage in the shortest time that he took a short cut through a gap in the blackthorn hedge that surrounded the aerodrome.

Whilst negotiating this gap he slipped on the ice, fell on his face and broke his nose. Instead of going to his billet he went to the sick quarters to have his injuries treated. When he explained what had happened he was put on a charge for 'breaking out of camp'. He should have gone out of the main gate. This must be a case of adding insult to injury.

During the time at Bicester I came to know a number of the under training Air Observers quite well. Names I can remember are Claude Hamilton, whose service number was next to mine, he was 581214 I was 581215. He was on the course at Sywell and at Aldergrove. Also Cyril Ankers, Charlie Ryan, John Dance, Arthur Avery and others. Although on different flights and different squadrons we all lived in the same hut.

During the course of lectures we were told about a big air battle near Heligoland in December 1939, where a large formation of Wellingtons had fallen foul of German fighters and suffered heavily. The RAF considered that Wellingtons with their four gun tail turrets flying in formation were invulnerable, the German fighters showed

71

otherwise. Some of the fighters the Germans used in this battle were Messerschmitt 110's. These two seater fighters were an unpleasant surprise sprung on us. The 109 we did know about but were always given to understand that its performance was not that good.

As the end of March approached the authorities considered we had been at Bicester long enough and it was time for us to move onwards. Accordingly over a period of a few days a number of us were posted to West Raynham to join 101 Squadron. Ryan had a car, a 1937 Jowett four seater saloon. He was driving this car to West Raynham and he invited Cyril Ankers and myself to travel with him.

While the snow was on the ground in February 1940 at Bicester the U/T crews spent much time just sitting waiting in the crew room (they also serve who only sit and wait). During that time I read a book entitled 'We, the accused', it was about fifteen hundred pages and the longest work of fiction I had read up to that time.

Most of the chaps played cards of some kind. Cards were always on the go. Whenever P/O Gilbert came into the crew room, before he took off his coat and hat, he would call out 'deal me in' to whoever was playing.

Soon after we arrived at Bicester the authorities decided the U/T Air-Observers needed to be inoculated. We needed five 'shots'. The MO had his five separate syringes lined up on his table. He fitted the needle to the first syringe, jabbed it into the arm and delivered the first shot. Leaving the needle in the arm he disconnected the syringe from the needle. The second syringe was then connected to the needle and the second shot delivered and so on, the needle being removed after the fifth shot. For a few days the performance of the observers arm was impaired when required to crank up the undercarriage of the 'Anson'.

CHAPTER FIVE

WEST RAYNHAM AND 101 SQUADRON
MARCH TO MID-MAY 1940

FOR LOCATION OF PLACES REFERRED TO IN THIS CHAPTER SEE MAP NO 4

List of illustrations etc. at the beginning of chapter 5

Map No. 4.

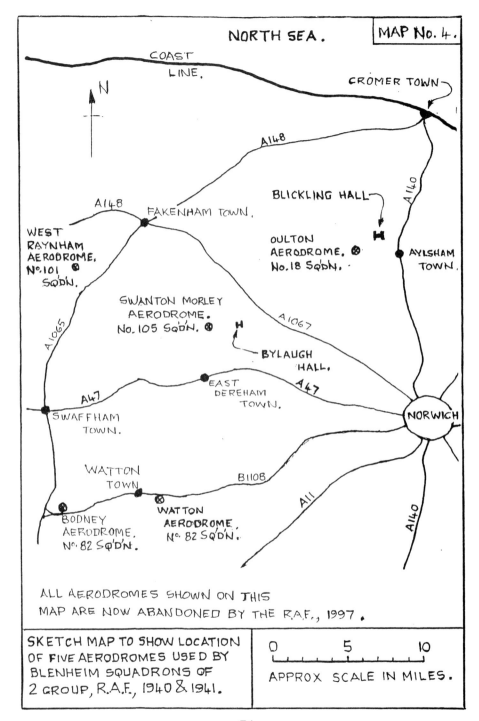

NORTH SEA.

MAP No. 4.

COAST LINE.

CROMER TOWN

N

A148

BLICKLING HALL

A140

A148

FAKENHAM TOWN.

OULTON
AERODROME.
No. 18 SQ'DN.

AYLSHAM
TOWN.

WEST
RAYNHAM
AERODROME.
No. 101
SQ'DN.

SWANTON MORLEY
AERODROME.
No. 105 SQ'DN.

A1065

A1067

BYLAUGH
HALL.

A47

EAST
DEREHAM
TOWN.

A47

SWAFFHAM
TOWN.

NORWICH

WATTON
TOWN

B1108

WATTON
AERODROME.
No. 82 SQ'DN.

BODNEY
AERODROME.
No. 82 SQ'DN.

A11

A140

ALL AERODROMES SHOWN ON THIS
MAP ARE NOW ABANDONED BY THE R.A.F., 1997.

SKETCH MAP TO SHOW LOCATION
OF FIVE AERODROMES USED BY
BLENHEIM SQUADRONS OF
2 GROUP, R.A.F., 1940 & 1941.

0   5   10

APPROX SCALE IN MILES.

I travelled from Bicester to West Raynham in the Jowett. The car must have been heavily loaded, three men plus kit bags. From memory it had only a twin cylinder, air cooled, horizontally opposed engine of less than a thousand cc capacity. The journey took us through Downham Market and was completed in daylight.

The aerodrome at West Raynham was all very new, having been open only about eighteen months. The sergeants mess and barrack blocks were all luxurious, plenty of space, central heating, high ceilings, large windows, parquet flooring etc. Added to all that it was the most glorious spring time, green leaves and blossoms bursting forth everywhere. The camp was in a very rural setting, the nearest town being Fakenham about seven miles away.

The squadron CO was W/C Hargreaves, he had flown Camel's in the Royal Flying Corps. I was assigned to 'A' flight, commander S/L Hartwright. Some of the chaps from Bicester were already there, others arrived within a few days. 101 was a 'pool' squadron, it was over strength with newly trained aircrews. Its purpose was to continue the training and to supply replacement crews to the operational squadrons in the UK and in France when they suffered losses.

Here we did practice bombing and air firing on the ranges at Wainfleet Sands on the northern shore of the Wash, south and west of Skegness. As at Aldergrove we dropped eleven and a half pound practice bombs (smoke). We bombed from six thousand feet, spotters in the two observation towers took bearings on the smoke and from these bearings the distance of the bomb from the target could be calculated see pages 40 and 41.

A flight of Battles fitted up for drogue towing was also stationed at West Raynham. These Battles flew up and down the range at Wainfleet while we fired at the drogue. Ground targets were set up in the shallow water near Wainfleet to be fired at by the air gunners from the turret and the pilots using the Browning fitted in the Blenheim's wing. The routine here was similar to Bicester. We all gathered in the crew room to await instructions. Any observer would fly with any pilot or W.OP.

The cross country flights were of longer duration than at Bicester, the outer tanks were filled. We did 'war load' take offs using the nine pound boost, and much formation practice. With the all new Mk IV Blenheim's, the luxury of the camp and the mess, the glorious spring weather, the fact that all the chaps were about twenty years old and had been selected for their physical fitness made life seem pleasant. At twenty one years old I was amongst the oldies, some were as young as eighteen.

When we had been at West Raynham about three weeks our friend Charlie Ryan was posted to the Middle East. This came as a shock to all of us, it was something we had not thought about. What happened to the Jowett I don't know. As well as the flying training, we did other twenty four hour duties, such as 'orderly sergeant' and 'guard commander'.

I remember travelling on the train from East Rudham, the nearest station, to Stamford. For some reason the train stopped while passing through an apple orchard near Wisbech, the beauty of the mass of apple blossom is beyond description.

On this journey we passed through much of England's geography and history. We saw the ancient town of Kings Lynn (we never did find out what happened to King John's baggage train), crossed the river Great Ouse, saw the RAF aerodrome at Sutton Bridge used pre-war as an armaments training camp. Much of this fenland was drained in the seventeenth century and was now used for sheep farming and vegetable growing, fruit growing around the ancient town of Wisbech. This district well known to the Norman's during their searches for Hereward the Wake.

Further west along the river Nene, approaching Peterborough, we pass large brickyards and in Peterborough much industry, engineering works, railway yards etc. On the north west outskirts of Peterborough the train passes Westwood aerodrome used during the war years as a flying training school.

Back at West Raynham near the end of April one of our number who had been with us all the time from Sywell was declared medically unfit due to migraine. He was discharged from the RAF and was given a civilian appointment in the newly formed Milk Marketing Board. In the idyllic surroundings at West Raynham the war seemed very far away.

For a reason that now cannot be recalled on April 9th I flew with F/Sgt Hill from West Raynham to Upwood. Whilst in the mess at Upwood at lunchtime we heard on the wireless that the Germans had invaded Denmark and Norway. This did not disturb the tranquil life at West Raynham.

On May 9th I was detailed as guard commander for a twenty four hour duty beginning at 16.40 hours. All the duties would parade on the parade ground under the command of the orderly officer. With some ceremony the ensign was lowered and the duties marched off, myself and about a dozen airmen to the guard room. From memory four sentries were posted at strategic points and these were relieved after two hours, so it was two hours on sentry duty then four hours in the guard room. At irregular intervals during the night the sentries were visited by the orderly officer. The guard commander stayed in the guard room for the twenty four hours.

On the morning of May 10th the BBC wireless told us that the Germans had launched an attack on Holland, Belgium and France. From the tranquillity of West Raynham this seemed of little interest to us. Over the next two or three days it was reported that the frontier barriers between France and Belgium were broken down to let the British army in France move forward into Belgium to engage the Germans. Movement forward of the army was hampered by floods of refugees fleeing away from the Germans.

We also heard the Germans were using parachute troops in Holland, thus by-passing the water defences. Also they were using troop carrying aircraft (JU. 52's). These aircraft landed on the North Sea beaches of Holland; the troops they carried then took the Dutch army by surprise and from the rear. Aircraft of the RAF attempted to strafe these aircraft when they were on the ground. Within days Holland and Belgium were defeated, the Maginot Line was outflanked and the German army applied all its attention to France.

On May 18th at about 18.00 hours the tranquillity at West Raynham was rudely shattered. A dozen replacement crews were to report to Watton, about twenty five miles away as the MT transport runs, by 21.00 hours. My name was on the list to go to Watton. At dusk that beautiful spring evening the two Bedford trucks from West Raynham pulled up outside the guard room at Watton and deposited thirty six laughing young aviators.

CHAPTER SIX

WATTON, BODNEY AND 82 SQUADRON
MID-MAY TO LATE-OCTOBER 1940

FOR LOCATION OF PLACES REFERRED TO
IN THIS CHAPTER SEE MAP NO 4 (CHAPTER 5)
AND MAP NO 5 (CHAPTER 9)

List of illustrations etc. at the beginning of chapter 6.

Legend on memorial stone.
82 Squadron Blenheims.
Sgt. Kenton and caption.
Outside the Sergeants' Mess at Watton in June 1940.

```
                    IN MEMORY OF

Wing Commander          Edward Colis de Virac Lart, DSO
Pilot Officer           Maurice Hardy Gillingham
Sergeant                Augustus Spencer Beeby, DFM

Pilot Officer           Earl Robert Hale
Sergeant                Alfred Edward Boland
Sergeant                Ralston George Oliver

Pilot Officer           Douglas Alfred John Parfitt
Sergeant                Kenneth Walther Neaverson
Sergeant                Leslie Reginald Youngs

Pilot Officer           Clive Warrington Wigley
Sergeant                Archibald Finlayson Morrison
Sergeant                Arthur Homer Pattchett

Squadron Leader         Norman Clifford Jones
Pilot Officer           Thomas Eckford Girvan

Sergeant                Cyril Ankers
Sergeant                Kenneth Victor Turner

Sergeant                Edward Victor Turner
Sergeant                Gordon Davies

Killed in action on a bombing raid to Aalborg Air Base,
the 13th of August 1940.

"No man is an island ... any man's death diminishes me,
because I am involved in mankind."
"And new life blossoms from the quiet sacrifice for
every man."
```

The above reproduction of the legend on a memorial stone in a cemetery near Aalborg, Denmark, is with the kind permission of Mr. Ole Rennest and Wartime Watton Museum.

Eighteen airmen of 82 Squadron R.A.F. were killed in action onAugust 13th 1940 when eleven Blenheims were shot down. Fifteen crew members, variously wounded, were taken prisoner.

The quotation at the bottom of the stone, "No man is an island ... mankind." is from John Donne (1573 - 1631).

82 Squadron Blenheims, Watton, 1940
Photo courtesy Wartime Watton Museum.

Sgt. Kenton of 82 Squadron, R.A.F., in May 1940 flying one of the Squadron's Mk.IV Blenheims on the circuit at Watton aerodrome.

These notes refer to the photograph of Sgt. Kenton opposite

Note the armour plate visible behind his right shoulder and the sliding perspex panel to his left which is pushed to the rear to give a clear opening. It was through this opening that the slipstream took Sgt. Brittain's helmet one night in September 1940, see pages 95/96.

On later aircraft a one piece "blistered" perspex panel was fitted such that the pilot could put his head into the streamlined blister to get a view to the rear.

The webbing straps over Sgt. Kenton's shoulders, perforated with brass eyelets, are part of his Sutton harness which retains him in his seat. The quick release pin for the Sutton harness is obscured by the pilot's right hand.

As Sgt. Kenton is not wearing a helmet or gloves or any other flying clothing he must be engaged on local flying only, climbing no higher than 1,500 feet.

The lighter coloured straps showing from under the Sutton harness is Sgt. Kenton's parachute harness.

Outside the Sergeants' Mess at Watton in June 1940

On the left John Dance, in the middle Arthur Avery and on the right Frank Harbord.

There was some excitement at Watton. The previous morning 82 Squadron had taken off to bomb the Germans now advancing in northern France and had been massacred by Me 109's. The effects and the billets of the thirty three missing aircrew had to be dealt with and accommodation had to be found for the new arrivals. Even the SWO was there to welcome us.

Next morning we reported to the squadron. We were welcomed by the C/O, W/C Bandon (the Earl of Bandon). 'B' flight commander was missing. Myself and others including Claude Hamilton were assigned to 'B' flight, F/L Hunt was to be promoted to S/L and flight commander. As a W/C he was to be killed in the summer of 1941 whilst attacking Tripoli harbour from Malta, shot down by an Italian CR42.

Replacement aircraft began to fly in, some brand new from the manufacturers. They had to be examined, tested, the squadron ident 'UX' letters applied. The squadron was required to be fully operational again on May 21st.

So on May 21st at 09.00 we assembled in the crew room, the squadron up to full strength in aircraft and aircrews. It was a glorious spring day. There was a grim silence all round, today it was for real not a jaunt down to Lyme Bay. The Me 109 had shown itself on a par with the Spitfire and the Blenheim had shown itself virtually defenceless. I was assigned to fly with Sgt Kenton, a pilot who had come up through the ranks. The name of our W.Op./AG I have no record or memory of. The Blenheim in those early days had one Vickers gas operated gun in the turret. From the description 'Gas Operated' the gun was known from its initials as a GO gun. The gun was fed by an ammunition drum containing a hundred rounds, a number of drums being carried.

During the afternoon we were transported by two-ton Bedford trucks to the Operations room in Station Headquarters. Here we were briefed by the Intelligence officer and the W/C. The Germans had crossed the Somme in the region of Abbeville and we were to attack them there. The training at Bicester now stood us in good stead, we were used to being hustled off the ground at short notice. All aboard the lorry to be transported to the aircraft. By the time we got to the

85

aircraft the C/O was there to tell us the operation was cancelled, return to the hangar to stand by.

The practice of storing the bomb sight in the armoury had now been abandoned, it was kept on the aircraft all the time. When the armourers loaded the bombs they also ensured the bombsight was fitted with the appropriate height scale. Likewise with the cameras, they were now fitted by the photographic section. All we had to do was level the camera, set the drift, and push the button at the appropriate time.

As it was now about 16.30 hours it was realised that if we were called upon for operations at dusk it would be dark by the time we returned to Watton. As a precaution parachute flares were loaded onto the flare racks. About 18.00 hours the 'tumbril' took us again to the ops room. The Germans had moved north from Abbeville and were attacking Boulogne. We were to attack them there. Due to the approaching darkness after the attack we were to break up and find our way back to Watton individually.

This time we did get off the ground, formed up in two boxes of six in line astern and set off for our target. We crossed the coast at Orfordness, and saw the balloon barrage at Felixstowe to our right. As soon as we crossed the coast we moved the bomb arming switch from 'safe' to 'live'. We then went out to sea to the Shipwash lightship where we turned south. As we approached Orfordness we could see three pillars of black smoke rising to a height of over a thousand feet. Looking at the map we could see these three columns stood over Ostend, Dunkirk and Calais.

The smoke was coming from blazing oil storage tanks. We could see the leaping red flames at the bottom, the whole towns appeared to be burning. During the next few weeks these columns of smoke were to become a familiar sight, indeed they came to be accepted as part of the normal landscape.

We delivered our bombs onto a concentration of German motor transport and armoured vehicles as we had been instructed. The return flight to Watton was via the same route as the outward flight. Arriving over the aerodrome at Watton there was still sufficient light to make a normal landing. The Me 109s had failed to find us, although we did have our first experience of flak which was not pleasant. We taxied up to the same parking place as we had started from and shut off. The ground crews were there to welcome us and to chock the wheels and lock the undercarriage.

We began to get out of the aircraft, collecting the navigation gear, maps etc into a navigation bag. I collected my parachute from under my seat where it had been stowed as suggested by Sgt Kenton for obvious reasons. We then started walking to the 'tumbril'* that was waiting on the tarmac. Some squadron aircraft had arrived home before us, others were still coming in. Ground crew took over the aircraft and began making their checks and inspections.

*NOTE The name tumbrill was used by the aircrew to describe any vehicle which was used to convey them from the operations room to the aircraft in which they were to fly. The name was used during the French Revolution to describe the carts used to convey the aristocrats to the guillotine.

Sgt Kenton said 'I've forgotten my helmet', as he was speaking he was turning and hastening back to the aircraft. The W.Op. and myself walked slowly on towards the 'tumbril'. Suddenly the whole area was illuminated from behind by a brilliant white light. We turned to look back towards the parked aircraft just in time to see Sgt Kenton staggering away from under the wing with his hand over his eyes. One of the ground crew had pressed the flare release button just as Sgt Kenton was passing under the wing. The flare had fallen at his feet, he almost stumbled over it, it had ignited instantly with such brilliance that when we got to him he was still temporarily blinded. The ambulance which was in attendance took him off to station sick quarters. The tumbril took us to the op's room where we reported what we had done and seen.

Newspaper reports began to talk of the B.E.F. making a 'strategic withdrawal to prepared positions'. We began to realise the allied armies did not have the wherewithal to halt the German advance. About this time the C. in C. of the allied armies in France, General Gamelin was replaced by another French General, this time General Weygand.

82 Squadron and other 2 Group squadrons continued to attack spearheads of the German army. We did not know it but a complete rout of the allied armies was going on in northern France. Royal Navy warships were attempting to pick up people from the docks at Boulogne, even although the docks were being shelled by the Germans. In an attempt to reduce the shelling 82 went to bomb the gun emplacements. Before we took off we were warned that the RN were treating all aircraft as hostile, it was up to us to keep out of range. As a luxury on this trip we were to have a fighter escort - twelve Defiants. We carried out the operation as ordered. In the vicinity of Boulogne our escort of Defiants drifted too close to the RN warships and were fired on, one of them being shot down.

About this time two all black Blenheims appeared parked on the aerodrome at Watton with the squadron code of WV, 18 Squadron. Also a number of 18 Sqdn airmen appeared having lost all their equipment and clothing in France. By the time all their lost kit had been replaced, the stores at Watton were stripped bare. All their squadron aircraft, tools and maintenance equipment had also been lost in France.

The weather was the most glorious springtime, blue skies and warm sunshine. Instead of sitting in the crew room we now sat outside in the sunshine on a warm grassy embankment. The squadron kept up its attacks on the advancing Germans as ordered. On one occasion eleven Blenheim's of 82 were joined by one of the all black aircraft of 18. All the aircraft of 82 were green and brown camouflage on the top surfaces, duck egg green on the underside. When crossing the coast returning to Watton a RAF Hurricane inspected us and decided the black Blenheim was a German intruder and without more ado shot it down.

As well as being home to 82, throughout this period, Watton was also home to 21 Squadron. They were involved in similar activity. Kites often came home suffering damage from shrapnel and bullets. If hydraulic pipes had been hit the undercarriage could not be lowered, 'belly landings' were not uncommon.

Sitting on our grassy mound one day we noticed the watch office windows were obscured by smoke on the inside. All the windows were then thrown open and the smoke billowed out, in a minute or two it was all cleared. Later in the day we heard the explanation. Our friend Cyril Ankers (with whom I travelled from Bicester to West Raynham) was on duty in the watch office. A few hours before we saw the smoke some sort of emergency had arisen with regard to an approaching aircraft and it was thought it may be necessary to 'warn-off' the aircraft from landing by firing a red cartridge from the Very pistol.

To be ready the appropriate cartridge was loaded into the Very pistol which was then laid on the table. A stranger came into the watch-office, picked up the Very pistol and squeezed the trigger. The red flare worked well; it made five or six high speed circuits around the inside of the watch office, giving off a cloud of smoke as it did so. It bounced off the windows, the walls, ceiling, floor, furniture and once off Cyril Ankers face.

To soothe the burns on Cyril's face the MO painted the burns with a healing ointment used by MO's as a cure all at the time, we always referred to it as gentian-violet. So for a few days Cyril walked about with a blue face. Luckily no permanent damage was done to anybody or anything.

Our bombing raids on the German army continued. One raid was in the area of Le Havre which we found to be also in flames similar to Dunkirk etc. with a similar column of black smoke. About the end of May a few survivors of the May 17th massacre arrived back at Watton. By fair means or foul they had flown across the channel in a heavily overloaded Anson. Amongst these survivors was a Sergeant Pilot named Watkins. The C.O. decided all the survivors should go on sick leave.

Permission was given by group (2 Group HQ) that Sgt Watkins and a Sgt W.Op. (whose name escapes me but who like Sgt Watkins lived in South Wales) could be flown by a squadron aircraft to the RAF station at St Athan. A sergeant-pilot named Bennet was authorised to fly the Blenheim with myself as observer and again an anonymous W.Op. to complete the crew.

We took off on June 3rd, a lovely summers day with a blue sky and a few tufts of scattered white fair weather cumulus clouds. About half way along the route the two pilots changed places so that when we landed at St Athan, Sgt Watkins made the landing although not authorised to do so. The landing was tail heavy and both pilots knew that damage had been done to the stern frame.

To avoid getting delayed at St Athan with an unserviceable aircraft it was decided that the two passengers would report the flight to the watch office and that Sgt Bennet and crew would take off straight away to return to Watton. Sgt Bennet made his take off run, when going at about 100 miles an hour and approaching the aerodrome boundary at a height of fifteen to twenty feet it became obvious the pilot had no elevator control. The heavy landing had cut the elevator control cables.

It was not possible to stop, so up undercarriage and hope for the best. The kite flew on straight ahead rising to a height of fifty to a hundred feet, enough to clear the trees. By gingerly experimenting with the trimming tabs and the throttles the pilot had a little control. By making a circuit about seven miles radius Sgt Bennet manoeuvred the aircraft back over the aerodrome where he closed the throttles allowing the aircraft to sink onto the grass and slither along on its belly. We were all relieved to be back on the ground, my feeling was that Sgt Bennet did a good job. We all returned to Watton by train.

About this time I was 'crewed up' with a Pilot Officer Hartley-Beavis, a very pleasant chap, we got on well together. Once a week the CO authorised a squadron crew to take a kite to Hendon and enjoy a day in London. Now it was the turn of Hartley-Beavis to enjoy this privilege. I had no particular interest in London whereas another sergeant observer on the squadron lived in London, so for that day he changed places with me. I never saw any of that crew again.

The story that came back from Hendon was that when they arrived a thunder storm was in progress with torrential rain. On his final approach the pilot's vision obscured by the rain, the Blenheim hit a concrete 'pill box' on the aerodrome boundary. The Sgt Observer was killed, Hartley-Beavis suffered broken legs and the W.Op. some serious injury. The observers name I remember as Jack Payne, remembered as a popular dance band leader on the BBC at the time had the same name.

By now the evacuation of Dunkirk was going on although we did not know it. The UK based Blenheims continued to attack the German army, the Daily Mirror talked about 'a wall of bombs to protect the BEF'. The Advanced Air Striking Force and the British Air Force in France (AASF and the BAFF) had ceased to exist about the middle of May. The Me 109 roamed the skies of northern France unchallenged, Ju 87s attacked the BEF all the time.

Despite all this intense action the weekly 'Wing Parade' still took place at Watton, the entire station strength forming up on the parade ground at 08.30 hours. These parades were instituted in peace time and were continued into the war years. The weekly 'Wing Parade' on a Wednesday would include the daily 'colour hoisting parade'. The parade would be inspected by the Group Captain. The RAF ensign would be hoisted, the Padre and the Group Captain would address the troops before we all marched off in column of route, the Group Captain taking the salute as we left the parade ground.

82 Squadron would march behind its own CO to the 'apron' between the squadron hangars, here all ranks would be addressed again by the Wing Commander before being dismissed to the days duties.

The squadron discipline Warrant Officer at this time was W/O Paisley. Individual airmen were discouraged from walking about the camp alone. Marching in small parties was the preferred arrangement, such that the Squadron became known as 'Paisley's 82nd foot'.

One Sunday morning in late June, at breakfast time, I met Sgt Brittain in the mess looking very tired and unkempt. He told me that the previous Saturday evening he had gone with others on a bus for an evenings entertainment in Norwich. By some miscalculation they had arrived back at the bus park after midnight and the bus had gone. There being no other means of transport at that time of night in the blackout they walked from Norwich to Watton, about twenty miles. This incident was to have a sequel in about January 1941 when we were stationed at Bicester (see Chapter 7).

Since P/O Hartley-Beavis suffered his accident at Hendon I was 'crewed up' with Sgt Brittain and flew with him on a regular basis until we were posted away from 82 Squadron.

82 Squadron was part of No 2 Group, Bomber Command. The group comprised about eight squadrons all based in the Norfolk/Suffolk area. The group commander in about June/July 1940 was Air Commodore J Robb. He kept in close touch with the squadrons by frequent visits. These were made by flying into the various aerodromes in his communications aircraft which was a Me 108. A small number of Me 108s were built to test the configuration of the airframe for the later Me 109. How the Air Force obtained this aircraft I don't know, it was said to have been captured.

One day in late June 1940 Sgt John Dance was on duty in the Watch Office. The ownership of the Me 108 was unknown to him at the time. This aircraft landed taxied in and parked near the Watch Office. As the pilot began to walk away from the aircraft, John opened a window and shouted down, "Hey, matey, what's your name?" He was embarrassed to receive the reply 'Air Commodore Robb from Wyton'. At the time 2 Group HQ was at Brampton Grange. The nearest aerodrome to Brampton Grange was Wyton.

One day when I was on duty in the watch-office some look-outs up on the roof called down 'a Hampden is coming over'. I rushed up the iron ladder and out onto the roof and identified the Hampden immediately as a Do 17 and saw him release his bomb load from a height of about two thousand feet. These bombs made a row of craters across the aerodrome. A party of airmen with shovels soon filled in the craters, the bombs did no damage to any aircraft or building. The next day one of our Blenheims taxied across one of these freshly filled in craters, the undercarriage leg on one side sank into the soft earth, damaging the undercarriage and a propellor.

I don't recall ever hearing any official announcement that the British army had withdrawn from France. About the middle of June the French capitulated and we were left to draw our own conclusions. During the second half of June individual aircraft were sent to attack targets in enemy, or enemy occupied, countries, the attacks to be carried out only if there was sufficient cloud in which we could take cover if Me 109's appeared.

To keep in practice we also did practice bombing at Wainfleet Sands. We had on the squadron strength a young Pilot Officer Keeble. One day he and his crew were detailed for practice bombing, his observer was Arthur Avery, well known to me from Bicester and West Raynham. The control office on the bombing range had a flagpole on the top from which a red danger flag was flown while practice bombing was in progress. After completing his practice bombing programme P/O Keeble came down to salute the control office and signal his departure from the range. Due to an error of judgement one of his wings struck the flagpole. The aircraft was immediately crippled, P/O Keeble went into a climb while he struggled to keep the wings level, all the time shouting jump jump jump. Arthur Avery clipped on his parachute, jettisoned the escape hatch, and jumped. When he jumped the aircraft was at about one thousand feet. As he hung in his parachute he saw another parachute floating down and the kite plunge nose first into a field and burst into flames.

When Arthur was on the ground and recovered his breath he bundled up his parachute and walked across the field to where he could see the other parachute lying. To his shock and dismay there was Keeble, still in his parachute harness but obviously dead. The W.Op. had 'gone in' with the kite. That evening I visited Arthur in the sick quarters at Watton where he was detained with a sprained ankle.

(P/O Keeble's father was also a RAF pilot as were his two brothers. One brother was killed on a Hurricane in the Battle of Britain, the other was killed whilst flying Faith, Hope or Charity in Malta and the father was killed in a flying accident in the UK in 1941. Four Keebles, all pilots, all killed).

In early July our good friend Claude Hamilton took off with his pilot, a P/O Smith, for a detailed reconnaissance of the channel Islands. What happened to them we never knew, they didn't come back. In the middle of July Arthur Avery went off again with another pilot on a cloud cover raid. Whilst flying below a sheet of cloud they saw a 109 turn onto their tail to make an attack. The Blenheim pilot pulled up into the cloud and made a ninety degree turn. After a few minutes in the cloud the aircraft was rocked by an explosion and the following conversation took place: Arthur 'Are we alright?': Pilot 'No, jump, jump, jump'. So again Arthur clipped on his parachute jettisoned the escape hatch and jumped. This time all three crew members landed safely but into the arms of the waiting German army and into a POW camp for the duration. Their aircraft had been hit by anti-aircraft fire whilst they were flying in cloud! The story of what happened to them was told to me by Arthur when I met him again in 1948.

The Squadron targets were now northern France, Belgium and Holland, particularly the Channel ports where reconnaissance had shown concentrations of barges. All this area was fiercely defended by flak and fighters. One photograph showing Dunkirk docks packed with barges was obtained by one of our Blenhiems at great risk, it was published in the press and the caption told the public it was from just a 'routine reconnaissance'.

About this time W/C Lart dropped instantaneous bombs onto Calais docks from three hundred feet and came home with his aircraft much damaged by bomb shrapnel, one hole through an outer wing panel was a foot in diameter.

The squadron did have a leave roster and Sgt. Brittain, was scheduled for a weeks leave from August 8th to 15th. In late July we began doing high level formation practice. The squadron would form up in two boxes of six around Watton and set off climbing westwards. We went onto oxygen at 10,000 feet and continued climbing to 20,000 feet. The formation would cross the Welsh coast at Aberystwyth turning in a big circle over Cardigan Bay. Then back over Aberystwyth still at 20,000 feet. Over Worcester, which we used as a turning point in both directions, we began a slow descent to land at Watton. Using Worcester as a turning point kept us clear of the defences around Birmingham. The formation was always led by W/C Lart.

W/C Lart was not as popular on the squadron as W/C Bandon had been. A Sgt Observer Robinson always flew with W/C Bandon. When W/C Lart took over the squadron he also took over W/C Bandon's observer and W.Op. Both these experienced airmen became increasingly uneasy about flying with W/C Lart, particularly after he dropped his bombs from too low an altitude at Calais. They made gloomy predictions about the squadrons future.

After we had done the high level formation practice over Cardigan Bay three times it at last came to the day for Sgt Brittain and his crew to go on their weeks leave. I spent the week at home at Little Casterton in the glorious countryside and the glorious weather. All too soon the week was gone and I returned to Watton. The first person from the squadron I met in the Sgts Mess was Sgt Robinson (the observer who flew with W/C Bandon and now flew with W/C Lart). He was surprised to see me, until he explained I didn't know why.

He then told me that on August 13th the squadron had taken off for a high level raid on the aerodrome at Aalborg in Denmark. Only one aircraft had returned, that of Sgt Baron, and he had left the formation about ten minutes short of the target when the squadron was still flying at five thousand feet. W/C Lart had found himself an officer observer to displace Sgt Robinson. Sgt Robinson did not mind leaving W/C Lart's crew but he was very upset at the loss of the squadron. Among those killed was my old friend Cyril Ankers.

I met Sgt Robinson again at Watton in May 1990 at a re-union. He was being pushed about in a wheel chair by his wife due to him having suffered a slight stroke a few months before. Sitting in his wheelchair he proudly wore his DFM and other campaign medals.

The squadron was in the process of rebuilding again. By the beginning of September the squadron had moved to Bodney about six miles west of Watton and W/C J.G. MacDonald was the new C/O. The squadron officers had their mess in Clermont House, about half way between Watton and Bodney. The Sergeants mess was in a farmhouse near Hillborough about two miles north west of Bodney. The domestic accommodation for the airmen was a group of huts half a mile east of the aerodrome.

Reconnaissance and cloud cover raids were still on the go, also the squadron was preparing for night flying. By mid September night flying circuits and landings were routine. Doing night flying circuits and landings with Sgt Brittain one night, he did not do up the chin strap on his helmet. When he put his head near the open panel to his left to get a view to the rear the slipstream took the helmet off his head pulling his inter-com jack out of its socket. The whole disappeared into the darkness of the night.

By the end of September the squadron was doing night operations mostly against the channel ports where large numbers of barges still constituted an invasion threat.

W/C J.G. MacDonald was a typical Cranwell trained officer with about twelve years service to his credit. He was always impeccably dressed and groomed and carried a swagger stick. The squadron also had a new sergeant discipline, a F/Sgt Yates, with about twenty five years service having enlisted in the Royal Flying Corps.

When in October we were told that Sgt Brittain* and his crew were to be posted to Bicester on 'rest' it came as a relief to me. The mess at Hillborough was never satisfactory, the night flying was very stressful. One night when the squadron was engaged in night flying about the end of September an aircraft flew across the aerodrome at about two thousand feet and dropped a number of bombs. No aircraft, personnel or buildings were hit. It was reported next day that the aircraft was a Whitley from 4 Group based in North Yorkshire, he was lost at the time he dropped his bombs and thought he was over northern France. About twenty airmen were on the aerodrome at night, they would carry out perimeter patrols and guard dispersed aircraft. These airmen used as a base a group of camouflaged bell tents. Each tent had been surrounded by a wall of sandbags built up to about three feet high. When the bombs from the Whitley exploded all the airmen, by good fortune or design, were in the tents and lying down. Thus, although the upper parts of the tents were riddled with shrapnel all personnel escaped injury. It was an excellent demonstration of the effectiveness of the sandbags.

* Since leaving Bicester in May 1941 I never heard of Sgt Brittain again until I read the book 'RAF Great Massingham' in about 1994 when I found him mentioned on pages 27 and 28.

CHAPTER SEVEN

BICESTER FOR THE SECOND TIME
& No.13 OPERATIONAL TRAINING UNIT.
LATE OCTOBER 1940
TO EARLY MAY 1941

FOR LOCATION OF PLACES REFERRED
TO IN THIS CHAPTER SEE MAP No 3 (chapter 4)

The Bicester of October 1940 was very different from the Bicester I had left in March. Both 104 and 108 Squadrons had departed elsewhere. The station was still doing the same job but was now organised as one unit and known as Number 13 Operational Training Unit. The station Warrant Officer was still the same (W/O Bucknell) but no sign of F/Sgt Devlin. The station commander was Group Captain Bowen-Buscarlet. Our paths were to cross again in about 1956 when he was a civilian working for De Havilland's northern factories.

The chief instructor on 13 OTU was W/C Sinclair who was to win a George Cross later for rescuing the crew of a crashed and blazing bomber. Sgt Brittain was posted to the flight that gave dual instruction to under training pilots, although on the same station we rarely saw each other.

The sergeants mess was grossly overcrowded, the whole place teemed with under training pilots, air-observers and W.Op./AG's. Being now 'screened' or 'staff' I sat with other screened crews in a 'staff' room adjoining the crew room, this period at Bicester is not well remembered.

One evening when I was sitting in the staff room a young pilot, Pilot Officer Verity, came into the crew room. He was detailed for two hours of solo night flying circuits and landings. He took off his fleecy overcoat and hung it on a hook on the crew-room wall. As he was getting into his flying clothing he was making jokes about things and then went out to his aeroplane. An hour later news came in that he was dead. He took off from Bicester and got mixed up with the Upper Heyford circuit. Upper Heyford, about four miles north-west of Bicester were also doing night flying.

He landed by mistake at Upper Heyford, on his attempted take-off he never got off the ground, he piled into the aerodrome boundary at about a hundred miles per hour. The kite was wrecked and he was killed. His fleecy overcoat hung there on the crew-room wall for a few days before his 'effects' were collected.

For night flying we now used a flare path made of 'glim' lamps. The 'glim' lamp was a cylindrical metal casing about seven inches diameter and about a foot high, the top being covered by a transparent perspex dome. Into the lower part of the casing a wet battery was fitted. Under the perspex dome an electric bulb gave out a subdued light. Under the perspex dome and over the bulb a metal shroud screened off the light such that it could only be seen by an airman flying at a thousand feet or less. The whole light system was mounted on gimbals in relation to the casing, the weight of the battery being sufficient to keep all the lighting assembly level at all times. The glim lamps were laid out in the form of a large T. The lamps would be laid about eighty yards apart. So if the upright of the T was twelve hundred yards long it would need sixteen glim lamps, the cross bar of the T being in proportion.

A pilot making a circuit at about a thousand feet could keep the flare path in view and would make his approach towards the bottom end of the 'T' and would land with the long element of the T on his port (left) side. For additional light, stationed near the landing end of the flare path was a powerful flood light. This device was mounted on a heavy trailer and was towed into position by a heavy lorry or tractor. Mounted also on the trailer was a petrol engine driving a generator to supply power to the flood light. If the pilot needed the flood light he would ask his observer to flash the letter F in morse code on the downward ident lamp when on his final approach, the flood light would then be switched on. Immediately after the aeroplane landed, when it was about a third of the way along the flarepath the floodlight would be extinguished.

These flood lights were made by the firm of Chance Brothers Ltd, the same firm that made lights and lenses for the Trinity House lighthouses. Because of the name of the manufacturing company these floodlights used by the RAF were always known as 'Chance Lights'.

I was to remain at Bicester until mid May 1941, in that time events took place that I can remember but cannot date or put in chronological order.

One day whilst walking across the apron I heard a number of loud heavy explosions away to the north-west. About six Blenheim's were on the circuit which was quite normal for those days. One of them was leaving a trace of black exhaust. As he approached to land two things seemed abnormal, one was he had no wheels or flaps. The other was that he did not follow the others to land across the middle of the landing ground, he was over to the side away from the hangars. Also he was going much too fast. All was explained in an instant when he opened fire on a number of Battles parked on the far side of the aerodrome. The shape of the fin and rudder confirmed it as a Ju 88. By this time he was on full throttle and away into the distance at low level.

We soon found out that the explosions I heard were bombs from the same Ju 88 dropped onto Upper Heyford aerodrome. After dropping his bombs he then found himself on the Bicester circuit, the Battles were a target he could not resist. Another time the station was visited and inspected by Lord Trenchard, I successfully avoided the inspecting party but was near enough to hear the celebrated 'boom' voice.

In late December 1941 an under training crew had got lost and had to land in a field near Cosford (Wolverhampton). The under training pilot made such a good job of getting the kite down undamaged in a very restricted field that experienced pilots agreed it could not be flown out unless some hedgerows were removed. A bowser from Cosford went out and refuelled the kite and a guard was posted on it until the ground was cleared to make enough room to take off. On new years eve Sgt Bullivant, myself and a W.Op./AG arrived at Cosford to fly the kite back to Bicester. How we got there I don't now know.

We went out to the kite by transport from Cosford. When Sgt Bullivant checked the fuel gauges he found all tanks empty. This caused great consternation in the camp, they would not refuel it again until the disappearance of the fuel had been investigated. The night of Dec 31st 1940, Jan 1st 1941 we spent in the 'Swan and Peacock' hotel in Wolverhampton. The flight commander told us to wait at Cosford until the kite was available.

So we waited Jan 1st, 2nd and 3rd and 4th. On the fourth an officer pilot arrived from Bicester to get things moving. It was 17.00 hours before he was given authority to take the kite, a 'Court of

100

Inquiry' was going on at Cosford. The officer pilot (F/O Aiken) arranged for glim lamps to be laid to indicate a take-off path across the fields. F/O Aiken had brought his own crew. We all piled into the kite, Sgt Bullivant, myself and our W.Op./AG sat in the 'bomb well'.

The 'bomb well' was the space in the fuselage between the two main wing spars. So with F/O Aiken at the controls the Blenheim thundered across the fields and rose into the pitch black night. The flight to Bicester was expected to be about twenty five minutes. After about 45 minutes the observer passed a note down to us asking if anyone had any idea of where we were. We had no idea. We could see nothing from the 'bomb well'.

After about another ten minutes droning on in the darkness the crew saw an aerial lighthouse and descended to below a thousand feet when they saw a glim lamp flare path. Much relieved they landed and enquired, it turned out to be Lichfield, a new aerodrome opened only a few weeks. After about an hours flying at 180mph we were about twenty miles east of Cosford. So we made a fresh start, took off from Lichfield and set course for Bicester. This time things went as expected and we duly arrived at Bicester. What happened and where we went on the first attempt only the observer and the Almighty know.

In mid January 1941 two or three crews went by motor transport to Aston-Down to pick up Blenheims allotted to Bicester. For this trip I was to fly with F/L Lascelles. We stopped in Cirencester for lunch, then on to Aston-Down aerodrome. F/L Lascelles was said to be the kings cousin, he went on to become a Wing Commander later in the year and met his death on one of 2 Group's low level operations. Aston Down aerodrome was in the vicinity of Cirencester.

In mid December 1940 with Sgt Bullivant I flew to Squires Gate, south of Blackpool. As we approached to land we could see lengths of drain pipe about six feet long and three feet in diameter standing up on end scattered along the runway. This made landing difficult. The watch office told us the drain pipes had been put there to stop aircraft from landing as the runway was not to be used. What we went there for I cannot now recall. When our business was done we took off again dodging the drain pipes. We flew over the Pennines dodging the defended areas around Manchester and Sheffield to the familiar scenery of West Raynham. Again I don't know why we went to West Raynham. As we arrived late in the day we stayed overnight.

What a difference now to the days of luxury in the spring of 1940. Where a bed had stood in the barrack blocks now stood a three tier bunk, the whole place seemed crowded and dirty. We were glad to get away back to Bicester next morning.

With Sgt Ratcliffe as pilot in mid-November 1940 I flew on an exercise around the Isle of Man. On the way back to Bicester Sgt Ratcliffe took the Blenheim along the Menai Strait and under the two bridges, both Telford's and Stephenson's.

One murky afternoon in December 1940 I was on the apron when out of the mist came a Defiant. When it landed and the pilot got out it was my old mate Sgt Kenton, he who had advised me to put my parachute under my seat at Watton in May. He was still troubled by his eyes but had been passed fit for daytime non-operational flying.

On occasions I flew with Sgt Costello-Bowen, a pilot who had survived the massacre of the 'Battle' squadrons in France in May-June 1940 with the Advanced Air Striking Force. Amongst other 'staff' observers was Sgt Tommy Broom who was to become well known later for flying with Sgt Ivor Broom, now Air Marshal Sir Ivor Broom KCB, CBE, DSO, DFC and two bars, AFC. Tommy Broom rose to be a Squadron Leader with DFC and two bars.

Other pilots names that appear in my log book are S/L Petley and F/L Langabear. S/L Petley was later W/C and CO of 107 squadron, he was killed on the Bremen raid in July 1941. F/L Langabear's name appears in the book of remembrance of those killed whilst flying at the RAF aerodrome at Oulton, he was on the strength of 18 Squadron. The book contains the names of over three hundred airmen killed whilst flying with various squadrons from Oulton. The book of remembrance is kept in the church of St Andrew at Blickling.

One Sunday morning in the Sergeants mess about January 1941, at breakfast time I met Sgt Brittain. He was unshaven and dishevelled, he looked as he had looked the Sunday morning at Watton when he had walked back from Norwich. A similar thing had happened, this

102

time he had walked back from Oxford in the blackout. On this occasion he was in good time for the bus. They did not get on board but stood talking near the back of the bus, the sound of the engine starting would be the signal for them to get aboard. The bus was parked on an incline and at the appointed time the driver released the hand brake and the bus rolled silently away down the incline. By the time the starting of the engine was heard the bus was fifty yards away, rolling about fifteen mph and intent on its journey. The walk back in the blackout this time was not quite so far but more difficult as sign posts had been removed due to the invasion threat. Finding the way back to Bicester under the circumstances was a feat of navigation and endurance worthy of some acclaim.

CHAPTER EIGHT

OULTON AND 18 SQUADRON
MID MAY TO EARLY JULY 1941

FOR LOCATIONS OF PLACES REFERRED
TO IN THIS CHAPTER SEE MAP NO 4 (CHAPTER 5)

List of illustrations etc. at the beginning of chapter 8.

S/L S. J. Monroe
Blenheim at Woodford
Congratulatory signal

Outside Blickling Hall (near Aylsham, Norfolk) Squadron Leader S.J. Monroe of 18 Sqdn. R.A.F. explains to the M.O. and the Engineering Officer how he attacked a ship in the North Sea from low level. His right hand represents the ships mast, his left hand the Blenheim approaching low on the water.

On the left of the photograph is P/O Eric Applebee D.F.M.

The photograph was taken in May 1941. At the time 18 Squadron were billeted in Blickling Hall but flew from the aerodrome at Oulton, about three miles away.

The photograph taken on 21st June 1941 is of an 18 Squadron Blenheim on the aerodrome at Woodford near Manchester (Avro's works). Standing on the step inside the front entrance hatch is Sgt. Frank Harbord, Air Observer.

Climbing down near the aft hatch is the 18 Squadron adjutant. The aircraft was flown from Oulton to Woodford by F/L. Thorne who also took the photograph.

To be inserted in D.R.O's.

The following congratulatory message has been received from the Air Officer Commanding No. 2 Group.

" The report received yesterday from the Photographic Interpretation Section of Bomber Command shows that the attack on a large Power Station in Northern France recently carried out by aircraft from Horsham and Oulton was most successful. It is certain that this Power Station will be out of action for some months to come, and this will have a big effect on the enemy's war production effort. I wish to congratulate the crews concerned and particularly the observers in leading aircraft on their accurate bomb aiming."

Stevenson

The above congratulatory signal was sent to the C.O. of 18 Squadron at Oulton in mid June 1941.
It concerns a 'circus' operation led by S/L S.J. Monroe D.F.C.
Aircraft number V6431 (Built by Rootes Securities Ltd.)
Crew: Sgt. Harbord, Observer, and P/O E. Applebee D.F.M., W.Op./A.G.

In mid May 1941 my second stay at Bicester came to an end due to me being posted to 18 Squadron at Oulton. The nearest railway station to Oulton, according to the official book in the Orderly Room, was Cawston. Both Cawston and Oulton are in Norfolk. Cawston being about three miles from the aerodrome at Oulton and about six miles from Blickling Hall where the squadron was billeted.

The train from Bicester took me to Cambridge on a lovely sunny spring day. At Cambridge there was a two hour wait for the train to take me on the next part of my journey. During that two hours, sitting in the sunshine, I read Somerset Maugham's book 'Carnival'.

The exact route from Cambridge to Cawston is now a mystery, but arrive at Cawston I did at about 19.00 hours. A telephone call from Cawston station to Blickling Hall brought transport to pick me up.

The next morning I reported to the squadron and met S/L. S.J. Monroe DFC and P/O Eric Applebee DFM with whom I was to fly.

The casualty rate was very high at Oulton as the squadron was engaged on low level shipping strikes. The low level strikes (altitude of fifty feet or less) were interspersed with high level (altitude ten thousand feet) raids over northern France known as 'rhubarbs' and/or 'circus's'.

Now on these high level raids twenty-four Blenheims would have an escort of over two hundred fighters, a close escort of twenty-four Hurricanes, and Spitfires and Hurricanes stepped up from five thousand to twenty thousand feet.

Life was difficult for the pilots of the Me 109's. Usually the RAF claimed about twenty German aircraft shot down. Our losses were light, the Blenheims usually returning unscathed. The pilots of the Me 109's had to content themselves with headlong dives through the Blenheim formations. It was a little disconcerting to see a Me 109, painted yellow from the spinner to the wing leading edge, standing on its nose about ten feet in front of your windscreen even although it was gone in a flash. The latest mark of Spitfire could outperform the Me 109 and was a match for the FW 190.

Before taking off on an operation from Oulton, which was a grass aerodrome, it was normal for the air gunner to test the guns in the turret. To do this the turret was turned to either the 3 o'clock or 9 o'clock position and the guns turned downwards to max depression such that the twin Browning guns were pointed almost vertically downwards. A short burst then into the grass would fetch up a clod of earth about eighteen inches diameter by about six inches deep.

All airmen billeted in Blickling Hall automatically became members of Blickling Park Golf Club with its course in the park. The greens were mown by a gang mower towed by a model 'T' Ford car. The model T remained in production until 1929. The car may have been only twelve years old but seemed ancient to us in those days.

While sitting in the sunshine at Blickling on June 21st 1941 the BBC announced that Germany, supported by Finland in the north and Romania in the south, had invaded Russia. So much for the friendship generated by the sacrifice of those Blenheims from Bicester in 1940. Also on the same day a Spitfire flew over with a cannon protruding from each wing, at least our fighters were now getting the fire power to surpass the Me 109.

One day at Oulton two Hurricanes landed and the pilots went into a conference with our squadron C.O. and flight commanders. One of the Hurricane pilots was the celebrated Bob Standford-Tuck who was to survive the war and to be much decorated.

The village pub in Blickling village was the 'Buckinghamshire Arms'. This was just a small village pub serving the local labourers and estate workers. It was frequented by the airmen. In the blackout it was all very dull, the interior being lit by dim paraffin lamps.

Pay parades were held in the stable yard of Blickling Hall. For a bet a New Zealand sergeant went up for his pay with his field service cap on back to front. While all his mates were on tenter hooks he marched smartly up to the table, received his pay, saluted, turned and marched smartly back to his place in the ranks. I suspect the paying officer would have noticed this irregularity but chose to ignore it.

We had church parades to St Andrews church in the Blickling estate. On the wall of the church is a memorial to some Harbord's who held positions of influence in the 18th-19th century.

On July 7th 1941 S/L Monroe was posted away on rest to a non-flying job. Myself and Eric Applebee were posted to 105 Squadron at Swanton Morley. These postings came quite unexpectedly, both Eric and myself were sorry to be separated from the pilot we had flown with on a number of operations over the past seven weeks or so.

CHAPTER NINE

SWANTON MORLEY, MALTA
& 105 SQUADRON.
EARLY JULY TO MID-OCTOBER 1941

*FOR LOCATIONS OF PLACES REFERRED TO IN THIS CHAPTER
SEE MAP NO.4. (CHAPTER 5)
& MAPS NO. 5,6,7, & 8.*

LIST OF ILLUSTRATIONS ETC. AT THE BEGINNING OF
CHAPTER 9:

105 Squadron.
MAP No. 5.
MAP No. 6.
MAP No. 7.
MAP No. 8.
Letter from Malta.
Citation, S/L Smithers.
Bylaugh Hall.

105 SQUADRON, R.A.F. SWANTON MORLEY, JULY 1941.

FRONT ROW: P/O. CHENEY D/O. DUNCAN F/Lt. LOVETT-CAMPBELL W/Cm. EDWARDS V.C. D.F.C F/Lt. BROADLEY P/O. APPLEBEE P/O. STANDFAST
P/O BRENNAN P/O. HANAFIN F/O. ROE S/Ldn. SMITHERS S/Ldn. GOODE D.F.C. P/O. RAMSAY D.F.C. P/O. SORENSON F/O. FRAYN

MIDDLE ROW: F/Sgt SAMWAYS Sgt BEMDALL Sgt KNIGHT Sgt BRUCE F/Sgt TAYLOR Sgt SCOTT Sgt SCHOLEFIELD F/Sgt SARGENT
Sgt NICHOLLS Sgt HARBORD Sgt QUINN D.F.M. Sgt FISHER Sgt MARSH Sgt HEALY Sgt HOARE

BACK ROW: W/O BROWN Sgt LYNDALL Sgt BROWN Sgt HINDLE F/Sgt KITTS Sgt JACKSON Sgt GIBSON F/Sgt BESWICK
F/Sgt LEAVESLY Sgt SMITH Sgt HILL F/Sgt TIMMS Sgt TUPPEN D.F.M. Sgt BASTIN Sgt FLETT

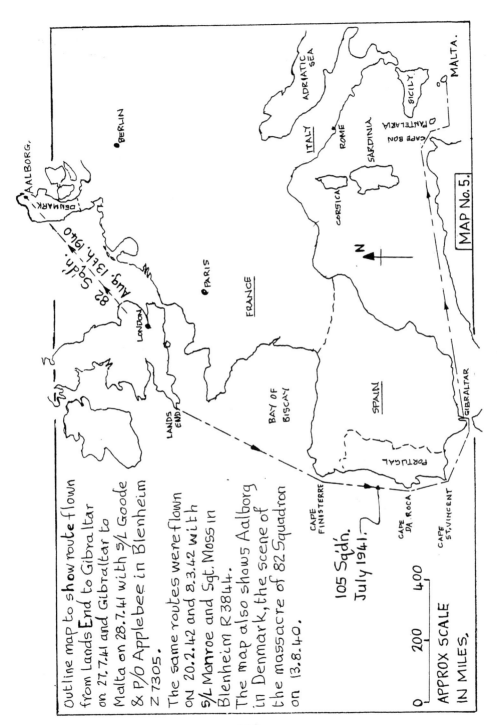

Outline map to show route flown from Lands End to Gibraltar on 27.7.41 and Gibraltar to Malta on 28.7.41 with S/L Goode & P/O Applebee in Blenheim Z7305.

The same routes were flown on 20.2.42 and 8.3.42 with S/L Monroe and Sgt. Moss in Blenheim R3844.

The map also shows Aalborg in Denmark, the scene of the massacre of 82 Squadron on 13.8.40.

105 Sq'dn. July 1941.

82 Sq'dn. Aug 13th. 1940

AALBORG.

DENMARK

BERLIN

LONDON
LANDS END

PARIS

FRANCE

BAY OF BISCAY

SPAIN

PORTUGAL

CAPE FINISTERRE

CAPE DA ROCA

CAPE ST. VINCENT

GIBRALTAR

CORSICA

SARDINIA

ITALY

ROME

ADRIATIC SEA

SICILY

PANTELARIA

CAPE BON

MALTA.

N

MAP No. 5.

0   200   400

APPROX SCALE IN MILES.

113

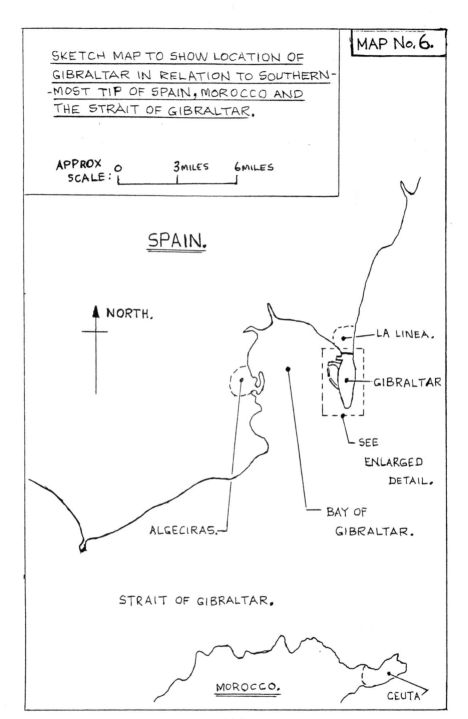

SKETCH MAP TO SHOW LOCATION OF
GIBRALTAR IN RELATION TO SOUTHERN-
-MOST TIP OF SPAIN, MOROCCO AND
THE STRAIT OF GIBRALTAR.

MAP No. 6.

APPROX
SCALE: 0   3MILES   6MILES

SPAIN.

NORTH.

LA LINEA.

GIBRALTAR.

SEE
ENLARGED
DETAIL.

BAY OF
GIBRALTAR.

ALGECIRAS.

STRAIT OF GIBRALTAR.

MOROCCO.

CEUTA.

114

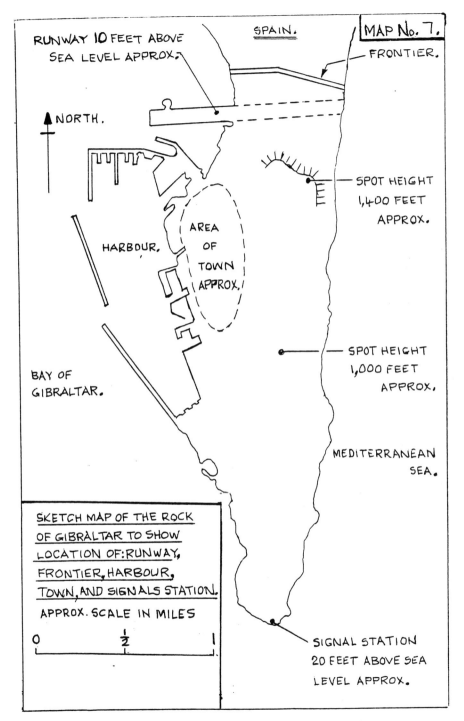

RUNWAY 10 FEET ABOVE SEA LEVEL APPROX.

SPAIN.

MAP No. 7.

FRONTIER.

NORTH.

SPOT HEIGHT 1,400 FEET APPROX.

HARBOUR.

AREA OF TOWN APPROX.

SPOT HEIGHT 1,000 FEET APPROX.

BAY OF GIBRALTAR.

MEDITERRANEAN SEA.

SKETCH MAP OF THE ROCK OF GIBRALTAR TO SHOW LOCATION OF: RUNWAY, FRONTIER, HARBOUR, TOWN, AND SIGNALS STATION.

APPROX. SCALE IN MILES

0   ½   1

SIGNAL STATION 20 FEET ABOVE SEA LEVEL APPROX.

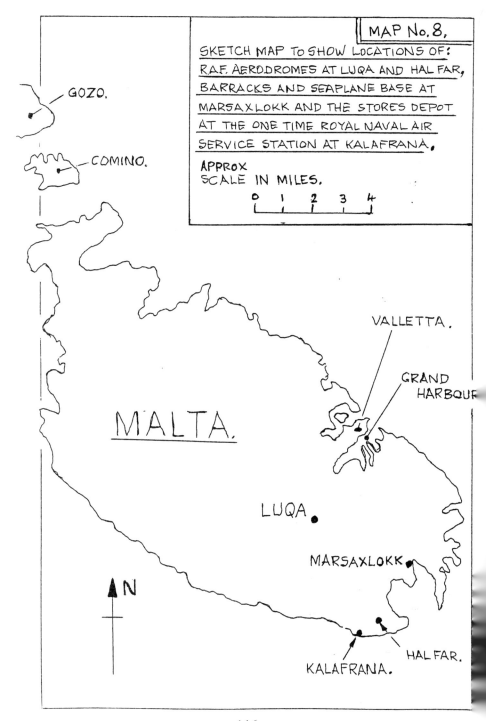

MAP No. 8.

SKETCH MAP TO SHOW LOCATIONS OF:
R.A.F. AERODROMES AT LUQA AND HAL FAR,
BARRACKS AND SEAPLANE BASE AT
MARSAXLOKK AND THE STORES DEPOT
AT THE ONE TIME ROYAL NAVAL AIR
SERVICE STATION AT KALAFRANA.

APPROX
SCALE IN MILES.

0 1 2 3 4

GOZO.

COMINO.

VALLETTA.

GRAND
HARBOUR

MALTA.

LUQA.

MARSAXLOKK.

N

KALAFRANA.

HAL FAR.

116

L-UFFIĊĊJU TAL-PRIM MINISTRU   OFFICE OF THE PRIME MINISTER

MALTA

L-Uffiċċju tal-Kabinett   *Cabinet Office*

3 September 1993

Mr Frank Alfred Harbord
43 Longcroft Lane
Welwyn Garden City
Herts AL8 6EB
UK

Dear Sir,

NATIONAL COMMEMORATIVE MEDAL

I have the honour to inform you that the President of Malta has been pleased to approve the Prime Minister's recommendation that "The Malta George Cross Fiftieth Anniversary Medal" be awarded to you. Your name will, in due course, appear in the List of Awards to be published in the Malta Government Gazette.

The Rules for the Award provide for the presentation of The National Commemorative Medal to be made by Malta's Representatives abroad in the name of the President. Award Ceremonies will therefore be held in London by Malta's High Commissioner.

Where it shall not be convenient or practical for the presentation to be made in person, the Medal may be delivered by registered post or such other means as may be considered expedient.

To facilitate the presentation arrangements, you are cordially requested to complete and tick as appropriate the enclosed blue card and to forward it, at an early date, to:

         Malta's High Commissioner
         16, Kensington Square
         London W8 5HH

Yours faithfully,

Miss C Attard,
Honours and Awards Co-ordinator

Enc.

AUBERGE DE CASTILLE, VALLETTA
TEL 225231, 220460; FAX: 244922

117

A.M. Bulletin No.5187.

ROYAL AIR FORCE AWARDS NO. 274.

<u>URGENT NEWS</u>

The KING has been graciously pleased to approve the following awards in recognition of gallantry displayed in flying operations against the enemy:-

Awarded the Distinguished Flying Cross.

Acting Squadron Leader Bryan William SMITHERS, No.105 Squadron.
In September, 1941, in an attack on Cotrone harbour, this officer obtained a hit on a 4,000 ton merchant vessel which subsequently appeared a total loss. In the course of a long patrol some days later, Squadron Leader Smithers observed two enemy ships. Attacking one of them he obtained a direct hit and left it in a sinking condition.

The next day, Squadron Leader Smithers lead a force of bombers which operated against a convoy of six merchant vessels escorted by seven destroyers. Flying through an intensive barrage, he successfully attacked the largest ship of the convoy. The vessel which was also damaged by other aircraft afterwards caught fire. Although his aircraft sustained damage Squadron Leader Smithers flew it skillfully back to base. This officer has at all times shown outstanding gallantry and fearless leadership.

Bylaugh Hall in its prime circa 1920's

The hall was used to accommodate N.C.O. aircrew in 1941/1942 when there was insufficient accommodation on the camp at Swanton-Morley.

The Hall was later used as the Headquarters of No. 2. Group R.A.F.
It is now partially demolished and in a ruinous condition.

P/O Applebee and myself reported to 105 Squadron at Swanton Morley on July 10th 1941, at about the same time the award of the Victoria Cross to W/C Edwards was promulgated. The atmosphere at Swanton Morley was very subdued due to the heavy losses. We did some training flights with S/L Goode, formation practice and practice bombing of a wrecked ship that was visible off Cromer at low tide. S/L Goode had suffered a bullet wound to his right hand a few months before, what had happened to his crew I don't know.

On July 16th we took part in the raid on the Rotterdam docks. A number of squadrons were involved, from memory 105, 21, 18 and 226, perhaps others. The role of S/L Goode was to lead out a squadron of Hurricanes from Coltishall to a D.R. position in the North Sea. This D.R. position was estimated to be on the track of the returning Blenheims. At the D.R. position we dropped a sea marker. The sea marker was to be a reference point which the Hurricane pilots could see and which they could circle until the Blenheims came along. We left the Hurricanes circling there and returned to Coltishall. About fifteen minutes later the Hurricanes returned and landed.

The Hurricane pilots reported the interception had gone well. The Blenheims had appeared in two groups, one just north and the other just south of the sea marker. The 109's that were expected to be in pursuit of the Blenheims did not show up. The Blenheims had suffered their usual losses over the docks, about 20%.

The next day we were warned to prepare to fly to Malta. We would stay in Malta for three weeks operations, leave our aircraft there and be brought back to the UK by Sunderland flying boat. It didn't work out like that.

Much work had to be done on the aircraft. Oil coolers and tropical air filters had to be fitted to the engines. Overload petrol tanks were fitted to the bomb racks. The earth camouflage, brown and green, was change to sea camouflage, grey and blue grey. The duck egg green of the undersides was changed to a tropical sky blue. Each aircraft was to carry a member of the ground staff, tools and spares.

The squadron took off from Swanton Morley late in the afternoon of July 25th, and formed up into two boxes of six. This formation then flew over the aerodrome at a height of a few hundred feet, dipping in salute over the Watch office where the Station Commander and other well wishers were assembled, and set course for Portreath (Cornwall). At Portreath we were to await suitable weather, as we could only undertake the flight to Gibraltar when we had a tail wind. At Portreath three or four mailbags were loaded onto each aircraft.

On July 27th the weather was favourable. Just before first light we thundered down the runway, when the nine pounds boost was brought in the exhaust collector rings around the front of the engines glowed red hot and blue flames about eighteen inches long were belching from the exhaust pipes. The full boost was needed due to the heavy load the aircraft were carrying.

From Lands End we set course for a point ten miles west of Cape Finisterre, climbing to an altitude of ten thousand feet. From that point we steered courses such that we passed Cape da Roca ten miles away on our port beam, likewise Cape St Vincent and Cape Trafalgar. Descending to a lower altitude we steered eastwards through the middle of the Strait of Gibraltar and approached the signal station on the southernmost point of the Rock from the south, at an altitude of one thousand feet. We identified ourselves by Aldis lamp from the nose of the aircraft and received a green acknowledgement.

The Rock of Gibraltar is at the southern end of a peninsular that projects southwards from the south coast of Spain. At the southern end of the Rock is a small flat area where the signal station is located. The Rock rises then steadily northwards over a distance of about two and a half miles to a height of fourteen hundred feet. The north face of the Rock is almost vertical. From the north face of the Rock to the barbed wire entanglement that marks the Spanish frontier is about a thousand yards. This narrow neck of flat land that joins the Rock to the Spanish mainland is about one thousand yards wide. The Rock itself widens out westward as you go south to a max width of about a mile before tapering away again to the southern point.

The flat area to the north of the Rock was in peace time a horse race track. When the war broke out this horse race track was taken over to be used as a landing ground. Obviously the runway had to run east and west. To increase the length of the runway material excavated from inside the Rock was dumped into the sea at the western end of the runway. By July 1941 this dumping had gone on for some time and had built up to such an extent that the runway was about fifteen hundred yards long.

After getting the green from the signal station we continued northwards keeping to the east of the Rock and well away from it to avoid the dangerous turbulence caused by wind flow over the Rock. At an appropriate position we turned west and flew over to inspect the runway on which we had to land. Then a circuit all the way around the Rock and make a landing approach from the east. After landing we parked the aircraft between the runway and the north face, parking space was very limited. The flight had taken seven and a half hours. Flying over the Bay of Biscay the observer transferred the petrol from the overload tanks on the bomb racks to the main tanks in the wings using a small 'Zwicky' hand pump fitted for the purpose.

It was a regulation on the rock that the first meal taken by newly arrived officers and NCO's be eaten in the mess with the 'men'. This must have been the case when we landed although I have no recollection of it. The NCO's were allotted to some bell tents as sleeping quarters. These tents were erected close to where the aircraft were parked. All the aircraft needed refuelling. This was done from four gallon tins. These tins were not reusable, they had to be broken open and the contents poured into a 500 gallon bowser.

The fuel was then pumped into the aircraft tanks using the engine driven pump on the bowser. The bowser being towed to the required position by any suitable tractor or lorry. As our bell-tents were in the area where all this work was going on it can be imagined that no one had much sleep. By 10.00 hours the next day we were all airborne flying eastwards towards Malta, pumping up the overload petrol again as we went along. Again we flew at ten thousand feet in good weather.

We kept over the sea, well away from the coast of north Africa, that was all enemy territory. Across the top of the Bay of Tunis we lost height in anticipation of getting under the radar screen that the Germans operated between Cape Bon and Pantellaria. So after Cape

Bon turn south at nought feet and remain at that height until it was estimated we were clear of the radar screen. Then eastwards again towards Malta. The islands of Lanosa and Lampedusa were seen clearly standing up out of the sea to the south on our starboard beam.

After landing on the runway at Luqa, the aircraft were dispersed as far away from the runway and each other as possible. Most of the ground crews were wearing steel helmets. Bombed down buildings were all around. The island was under siege. The operations room was underground. We were sent to billets at the old Royal Naval Air Service station at Marsaxlokk. This was about ten miles from Luqa and had suffered little from the bombing. During the first week we were there we discovered a 'Sunderland' flying boat was sunk in the bay. The water was about fifteen feet deep, the 'Sunderland' was standing on the bottom on an even keel the right way up. The water in the bay was clear (in 1941) such that when we swam we could see the Sunderland and could dive and touch its wings.

The flying boat had alighted, unloaded and then been sunk by cannon fire from a Me 109 while at its mooring. A slip-way led up to a large hard standing in front of an aircraft hangar. We discovered the hangar housed a captured Heinkel 115, a large twin engined float plane. This aircraft was being made serviceable by RAF mechanics. Sometimes a 'Walrus' would come and alight on the water, lower its wheels, taxi to the slipway and taxi up the slipway and onto the hard standing.

RAF launches plied between Marsaxlokk and the other old RNAS station at Kalafrana. Much of what I believed went on at Marsaxlokk is based only on hearsay and rumour. The RAF launches would also deliver and collect intelligence agents to and from the north African coast. We watched these men in civilian dress embark and disembark on the launches, we could not verify who they were or where they went.

The squadron at Luqa before us was 110 from Wattisham. Their C/O, W/C Hunt had been shot down and killed over Tripoli by an Italian CR42, he had been my flight commander on 82 Squadron at Watton in May 1940. A F/L Watkins had come back from an operation in a badly shot up Blenheim. He was very seriously wounded in the leg. This was the same Watkins who as a Sgt Pilot had been shot down on May 17th 1940 with 82 Sqn and with whom I had flown to St Athan on June 3rd 1940.

110 Squadron had suffered severe losses in their ops from Malta. We used a partly demolished building at Luqa as a crew room. Above the doorway a departing member of 110 had put a notice, 'Abandon Hope all ye who enter Here' followed by 'Welcome to 105 Squadron, and how'. ('And how' was a popular expression at the time, originated in the USA).

105 Squadron arrived in Malta on July 28th and were in action the next day. On August 3rd S/L Goode, myself and Eric Applebee led eight aircraft on a low level raid on shipping in Tripoli harbour at dusk, we got away without loss. After the attack the formation split up and flew back to Malta individually in the dark.

About the middle of August I was admitted into the British Military Hospital suffering from Sand Fly Fever, this kept me away from the squadron for about ten days. During convalescence I wore (like all the others) 'hospital blues'. This was a uniform of easily washable navy blue trousers and jacket, white shirt and red tie.

While I was in hospital S/L Goode, P/O Applebee and Sgt Nichols were shot down and taken prisoner during a raid on an explosives factory at Cotrone on the Italian mainland south of the Gulf of Toranto. When I came out of hospital I flew with our other Flight Commander S/L BW Smithers.

Before 105 Squadron arrived in Malta the island had been heavily bombed by the German air force, this bombing was now much reduced as the Germans needed all their aircraft to support their attack on Russia. Desultory bombing did go on at night by the Italians.

Also based at Luqa were a number of RAF 'Marylands', these aircraft kept up a high level reconnaissance to the east and west of the island. No ships made the crossing from Italy to North Africa that we did not know about. Any ships seen by the 'Marylands' would be attacked by Blenheims, Swordfish and submarines.

My 23rd birthday on September 12th 1941 was another lucky day for me. On that day, flying with S/L Smithers we led out eight Blenheims to attack a convoy making for Tripoli. The convoy consisted of five merchant ships and seven destroyers.

Before take off S/L Smithers had decided that on this trip he would drop the bombs himself. A bomb release button had been arranged on the control 'spectacles' convenient for the pilots right thumb. When we were within about five miles of the convoy the first half of my job was done. I remember saying to the S/L 'there she blows', moving back from the plotting table to the seat beside the pilot and putting my lap belt on.

S/L Smithers selected the biggest merchant ship as his target and began his run in. As we neared the ship he pulled down the nine pounds emergency boost lever. My role during the attack was to be just a spectator, I would see what no-one else would ever see and only those who have taken part in similar attacks can imagine. The anti aircraft fire was intense. When about five hundred yards from the ship a glance at the pilots instrument panel showed both engines were giving max revs, the airspeed indicator was showing 230mph, altimeter reading zero. A glance then at the total concentration showing on the pilots face. It was a surprise to see a tear trickling down both of his cheeks.

At that instance he would be considering many factors, the size of the ship, the height of the rigging and masts, the speed of the aircraft, when to press the bomb release, how the bombs would skip, when to pull the Blenheim up to get over the masts and rigging. Despite the reading of the air speed indicator it seemed we were standing still and being shot at by all the guns in the world.

Then came the banging shut of the bomb doors and the downward pressure on the seat as the stick was hauled back followed by the negative 'G' force as the stick was pushed forward, we were over the rigging and still alive. It was then that I realised tears had also been trickling down my cheeks.

A glance to the right showed a Blenheim burning furiously as it cartwheeled through the air to crash into the sea.

The phenomenon of involuntary tears has never been mentioned before to anyone. I never mentioned it to S/L Smithers. At the time our thoughts were totally occupied with the job in hand. In the many books about RAF operations that I have read it has never been mentioned and it was only on this occasion that I observed it. My explanation to myself is that it was a natural reaction to the stress we were under.

From over the rigging forward pressure on he stick took us down to the 'safety' of the wave tops. All the time the engines running at nine pounds boost were carrying us further away from the convoy. At the speed we were going three minutes would take us over ten miles. The engine boost pressure was then returned to normal. Another Blenheim came along on our starboard side and for a minute flew in formation with us, it then without warning turned at right angles away from us and plunged into the sea. We circled to see the three crew members climb aboard their dinghy.

Of the eight Blenheims that took off, five, all damaged, returned. The position of the dinghy was reported. W/C Edwards contacted the RN and the submarine HMS Utmost was sent out to pick up the survivors. Next morning sergeants Brandwood, Miller and Mee, sitting in their dinghy were surprised to see a periscope come up out of the water and move towards them. They were relieved when it turned out to be British. The submarine carried them back to Malta.

At that time Blenheims were being flown out individually to the middle east as reinforcements. To keep up the strength of the squadrons based on Malta these transit aircraft and their crews were sometimes 'shanghaied' and taken onto the squadron strength. At this time, September 1941, 107 Squadron also had a detachment of Blenheims at Luqa. As we all lived at Marsaxlokk and dined in the same sergeants mess, track was lost of who was on the strength of which squadron.

Having been engaged on low level flying over the sea for some months the observers had become expert at navigating under these circumstances. It had been found that by closing one eye, three quarter closing the other and squinting through the bombsight, 'speed lines' could be seen on the surface of the water. By bringing the drift wires of the bomb sight parallel to the 'speed lines' a very accurate measure of the aircraft drift could be found.

We had also become expert at estimating the wind speed by the state of the 'white horses' on the wave crests. Absence of 'white horses' was an indication of light winds. By looking at the surface of the water from a height of fifty feet or so we could recognise the 'wind lanes' on the water, these also gave a good indication of wind speed and direction. We became very confident at finding our way about the trackless ocean. These methods of finding the wind were not in the navigation manual (AP1234). The wind speeds and directions that we found by our own methods were often at variance to those given by the met. forecasts, the met. forecasts were often duff. As an example, for the raid on Tripoli docks, August 3rd, the met wind was something like a hundred and twenty degrees different in direction to the wind we found.

The brewery on Malta was still brewing beer in 1941. The name of the brewery was 'Farson's'. The various grades of beer they produced were denoted by different coloured labels on the bottles. Farson's Blue was always favourite amongst the airmen.

In 1942 the King, George VI, announced the award of the George Cross to the island of Malta. In 1992 the President of Malta GC, on the fiftieth anniversary of the announcement of the award of the GC, announced the award of a commemorative medal to all members of the armed forces who served in Malta GC during the siege. The siege began in June 1940 and was not lifted until July 1943 after the invasion of Sicily.

Authority to wear the Malta George Cross Commemorative Medal on the same level as those medals awarded by the Crown is contained in the London Gazette of April 15th, 1992.

CHAPTER TEN

CRUISING WITH THE ROYAL NAVY
AND RETURN T0 SWANTON MORLEY
MID-OCTOBER TO MID-NOVEMBER 1941

FOR LOCATIONS OF PLACES REFERRED TO IN THIS CHAPTER SEE MAP NO. 5 (CHAPTER 7) & NO. 4. (CHAPTER 5).

List of illustrations etc. at the beginning of Chapter 10.

Supermarine "Walrus".

Supermarine "Walrus" amphibious maritime reconnaissance aircraft. Two aircraft of this type were carried aboard the heavy cruiser H.M.S. Edinburgh in 1941. They were launched from the ship as required by catapult and later recovered (after alighting on the water) by crane. Reproduced with kind permission of Comm Squadron Aviation Photos.

One Saturday evening in mid October at about 20.00 hours S/L Smithers and two or three other 105 officers turned up at the Sergeant's mess at Marsaxslokk in a car. In the car boot they had some crates of Farsons blue. They told us that a convoy was coming into Valletta at first light and that we were to be on the dockside at 07.00 hours on the Sunday morning to be conveyed back to the UK.

We were on the dockside at the appointed time together with many other service people, army and navy as well as RAF. All around and at every vantage point the Maltese had gathered. Then the first ship appeared steaming slowly and majestically into Grand Harbour. I think it was the heavy cruiser, HMS London. The Royal Marines band was up on the foredeck playing, 'Here we are again'.

As the ship steamed slowly in the local Maltese cheered, waved and wept. The British kept a stiff upper lip. This first ship was followed by others, cruisers and destroyers of the RN and merchant men all steaming grandly in to their allotted berths. All anti-aircraft guns were manned and pointed skywards as bombing raids were expected. We were notified that we were to travel on HMS Hermione, a 5,000 ton anti aircraft cruiser. Her main armament was 5.25 inch anti aircraft guns. These guns were made in Czechoslovakia. As well as being anti aircraft guns they could be used as normal navy guns. We also found out that the convoy had a very hard time on the way from Gibraltar.

It had been constantly attacked from the air. A number of ships had been sunk. The battleship HMS Nelson had been hit by torpedo and had to return to Gibraltar down by the bow. The convoy had shot down a number of enemy aircraft. The warships that had escorted the convoy from Gibraltar were known as 'Force H'. The warships that escorted the merchant men into Malta were detached from 'Force H', the main body of which had been left steaming about Cape Bon. To cause a distraction while the merchant men made their run into Malta 'Hermione' steamed south and shelled Pantellaria from the south. The shell cases, brass tubes about six inches diameter at the small end and tapering to eight or nine inches diameter at the large end were all stood up together on end on the ships deck, restrained by netting from falling overboard. The shell cases were about four feet long. All that Sunday 'Hermione' lay in the Grand Harbour, at action stations, no enemy aircraft appeared.

Soon after dark Hermione crept quietly out of the Grand Harbour turned north and increased speed. Crew members told us they were running at full speed, at 35 knots. About five miles off the coast of Sicily the ship turned to north-west and steamed along parallel to and about five miles off the coast of Sicily. In the morning a most glorious and majestic sight. While I had slept Hermione had rejoined Force H (and presumably all the other warships that had gone into Malta had also rejoined Force H).

This fleet of warships far exceeded anything I had ever imagined. The sea was calm and the sky blue. The battleship 'Rodney' was to the fore followed by perhaps four other battleships one of which was 'Malaya' (the 'A-K' line?). With them was the aircraft carrier 'Ark Royal'. Around these ships steamed say eight heavy cruisers (10,000 tons, 6 inch guns) then the same number of light cruisers (5,000 tons 5.25 inch guns) of which Hermione was one. All screened by about thirty destroyers.

On the journey westwards the ships carried out various exercises. A flight of 'Fulmar' aircraft from 'Ark Royal' kept up a patrol overhead all the daylight hours. 'Swordfish' rumbled off and on the deck of 'Ark Royal' at intervals. The surrounding destroyer screen carried out depth charge attacks on submarines, real or imaginary we could not tell. One of the cruisers would steam off to act as a target for the battleships guns. The target ship would steam along at the same speed as the battleships and on the same course about five miles away. The gunners on the battleships would fire to drop their shells about half a mile behind the target ship.

During the voyage to Gibraltar no enemy aircraft appeared. The ships must have arrived in Gibraltar during the Tuesday night. During the Wednesday the ships were refuelled and we, a small group of about six airmen, were transferred to HMS Edinburgh, a heavy cruiser of ten thousand tons with six inch guns. During the Wednesday night 'Edinburgh' sailed from Gibraltar and headed westwards into the Atlantic. After two or three days Edinburgh met four merchant ships, the five ships then steamed in company northwards.

After some days steaming northwards the convoy turned east to make for Greenock. 'Edinburgh' had two 'Walrus' aircraft on board, bi-plane amphibians. The Walrus had a single engine with a pusher propellor and foldable wings. When the wings were folded the aircraft were stowed in tight fitting hangars on deck. The aircraft were launched by a catapult mounted across the ship. The catapult was powered by an explosive charge as used to fire a shell from the six inch guns.

We always watched with great interest the launching and recovery of these aircraft. The aircraft was loaded onto the catapult, the crew went aboard and the engine was started. When the crew were satisfied they took up their positions for the launch. The crew disappeared into the aircraft hull, the pilot sat in his seat with his head pressed against his head rest and ran the engine up to full power. When all were satisfied the engine was OK at a signal the charge was fired with a great bang and a cloud of smoke. The aircraft just disappeared and then could be seen three or four hundred yards away from the ship and skimming just clear of the water. Very slowly it would gain speed and height and be lost to sight in the distance. The 'Walrus' looked tiny in the vastness of the mid Atlantic.

After an absence of four or five hours a tiny speck would appear in the sky. The speck would grow into the Walrus. Edinburgh must have stopped so that the Walrus could alight alongside. Then followed the hair raising spectacle of hoisting the Walrus back on board. The Walrus would be wallowing in the water and Edinburgh rolling in the swell. A crane would be run out over the side of the ship projecting about 25 feet. On the outboard end of this crane was a pulley and over the pulley dangled a cable with a hook on the end. The hook was lowered towards the Walrus. A crew member on the Walrus would stand up in the front gun turret and with a boat hook try to get a hold of the dangling and swinging cable.

The Walrus must have been fitted with a lifting eye above the top wing and at the centre of gravity. When the Walrus crew had succeeded in capturing the cable the hook would be engaged in the lifting eye and the Walrus hoisted on board. This was all a most hazardous operation. Having done plotting exercises on admiralty charts we were well aware of the difficulties of finding the ship after being away for four or five hours; it being necessary for the ship to alter course and speed to foil any possible submarine attacks.

The procedure of launching and recovering a Walrus went on twice a day, once in the morning and once in the afternoon. If the weather was rough when the Walrus appeared the following action took place. Edinburgh would steam into wind at speed for a distance of say a mile leaving a smooth wake. The ship would then do a smart 180 degree turn and slow down and stop alongside her wake which would still be visible in the water. The Walrus would then alight on the smooth water of the wake and be hoisted aboard in the normal manner.

We would watch with bated breath as the Walrus crew captured the swinging cable. It always seemed a miracle they did not fall overboard. No doubt they were tethered to the Walrus by a monkey buckle. Exactly what the merchant ships did while all this went on I can't recall, presumably they stood off at a safe distance out of the way.

We were billeted in a small mess of petty officer mechanicians. These were all chaps of mature age, say in their forties, with twenty years or more experience in the service. They treated us as guests and did everything they could to make us comfortable. When 'off watch' they would play 'Mar Jong', a most complicated and lengthy game that I could never understand. During daylight off duty hours they would walk up and down on the ships deck for exercise. After about twelve days on board, Edinburgh delivered her clutch of merchant men safely into harbour at Greenock.

Customs men came aboard searching for contraband, mostly silk and tobacco. Customs were treated with great respect by the sailors. We had docked at about eight o'clock am and went ashore at about two o'clock pm. S/L Smithers made all the arrangements for us. We went by train to Glasgow. We must have waited on the station, in due course we caught the over-night express to London, presumably to Euston.

From Euston we went to the Union Jack Club for breakfast and wash and brush up. After the ablutions when I put my tunic on I noticed the button on the left breast pocket was undone, I did the button up and thought nothing of it. From the Union Jack Club we went to Liverpool Street station to get the train to East Anglia; we were making for our base at Swanton-Morley. On the train, for reasons I cannot now recall, I went to my left breast pocket for my wallet. To my horror and dismay my 'Irish Jaunting Cart' wallet was gone, stolen in the Union Jack Club. The wallet I had bought while we were under training at Aldergrove, it contained fifteen pounds (about three hundred pounds at today's value) and a dozen cuttings from the 'Malta Times' reporting activities carried out by 105 in Malta.

We arrived at Swanton Morley to find our billets in the sergeants mess had been taken over by others, our kit that we had left in the billets (we were only to be away three weeks) had been collected and put into stores. The only billets that could be found for us were in Bylaugh Hall about two and a half miles away from the mess. In the morning, up bright and early and walk to the mess for breakfast then report to the crew room. There we found the squadron had a new C/O, W/C Simmons, and two new flight commanders. One of the new flight commanders was S/L Jesse Oakshott, who I had met various places before in 2 Group. Blenheims still stood around the dispersals, the squadron was not operational. It was being reformed and was awaiting delivery of De Havilland 'Mosquito' aircraft to replace the Blenheims. All the old Blenheim crews were super-numeries. We kept our hand in with the usual training on the Blenheims.

The new C/O assured us there was no chance of Blenheim crews being retrained to fly the Mosquito and that in due course we would all be posted. In the middle of November 1941 the first Mosquito was delivered to Swanton-Morley by Geoffrey De Havilland junior. By the end of the month all the survivors from Malta had been posted. S/L Smithers was posted to a Stirling squadron; I was posted to 14 OTU, Hampden's, at Cottesmore.

CHAPTER ELEVEN

COTTESMORE AND NO. 14
OPERATIONAL TRAINING UNIT
MID-NOVEMBER 1941 TO
MID -JANUARY 1942

*FOR LOCATIONS OF PLACES REFERRED
TO IN THIS CHAPTER SEE MAP* No. 9.

List of illustrations etc. at the beginning of Chapter 11.

Map No. 9.
Landmark beacon.

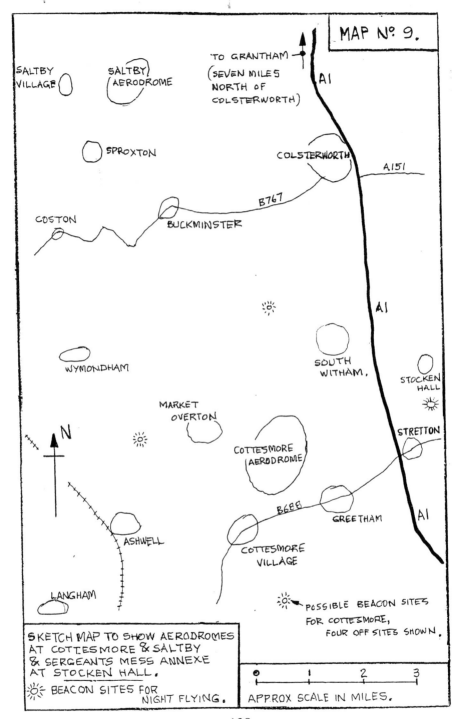

MAP No 9.

SALTBY VILLAGE

SALTBY AERODROME

TO GRANTHAM (SEVEN MILES NORTH OF COLSTERWORTH)

A1

SPROXTON

COLSTERWORTH

A151

B767

COSTON

BUCKMINSTER

A1

SOUTH WITHAM.

WYMONDHAM

STOCKEN HALL

MARKET OVERTON

STRETTON

N

COTTESMORE AERODROME

ASHWELL

B688

GREETHAM

A1

COTTESMORE VILLAGE

LANGHAM

POSSIBLE BEACON SITES FOR COTTESMORE, FOUR OFF SITES SHOWN.

SKETCH MAP TO SHOW AERODROMES AT COTTESMORE & SALTBY & SERGEANTS MESS ANNEXE AT STOCKEN HALL.
BEACON SITES FOR NIGHT FLYING.

APPROX SCALE IN MILES.

138

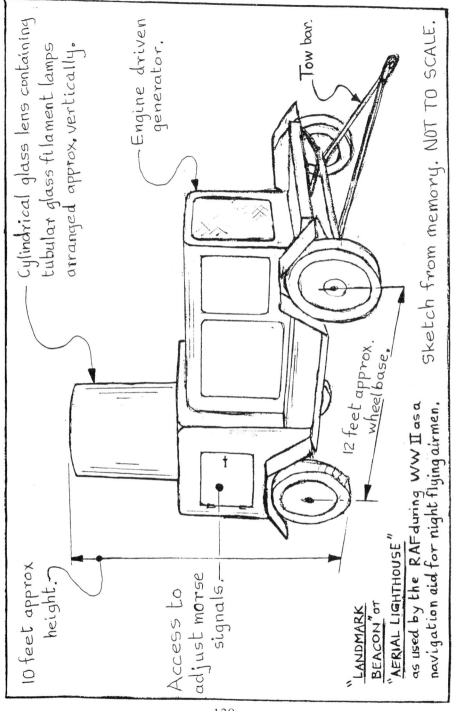

Cylindrical glass lens containing tubular glass filament lamps arranged approx. vertically.

Engine driven generator.

Tow bar.

10 feet approx height.

Access to adjust morse signals.

12 feet approx. wheelbase.

"LANDMARK BEACON" or "AERIAL LIGHTHOUSE" as used by the RAF during WW II as a navigation aid for night flying airmen. Sketch from memory. NOT TO SCALE.

The small, stone built, village of Cottesmore in Rutland (England's smallest county) gives its name to the nearby RAF aerodrome as well as to a pack of well known fox hounds. When I arrived at the aerodrome during the last week of November 1941 the sergeants mess was situated in the camp on the aerodrome, with an annexe at Stoken Hall, a large country house, about four miles away to the east-north-east. People were transported between the mess proper and the annexe by motor lorry.

The aerodrome was home to number 14 Operational Training Unit (14 OTU), engaged on training Hampden bomber crews for Bomber Command. As well as Hampdens the unit had a number of Ansons. These aircraft were dispersed around the aerodrome at Cottesmore and also at the satellite landing ground at Saltby. Saltby was about eight miles NNW of Cottesmore and had virtually no accommodation for airmen, just a few wooden huts for the aircraft servicing crews. The flying crews were transported to Saltby from Cottesmore when required by motor lorry.

Most of the flying at Cottesmore was done at night, whatever the weather. After about two weeks at Cottesmore we heard the news of the infamous Japanese attack on Pearl Harbour. The war had been going for two years and three months and we were used to bad news, a bit more didn't seem to make much difference. Anyway we had been assured over the years that Japanese equipment was sub-standard, they were incapable of making anything original. We had our 'Gibraltar of the Far East' at Singapore. The Royal Navy could hold the fort while we dealt with the real enemy, Germany.

Sometimes I was detailed to fly with under-training crews to oversee the work of the observer. The morning after a programme of night flying it was quite normal to see a couple of Hampdens pranged on the aerodrome or about its boundaries.

One flight at Cottesmore that I was involved in is retained in my memory. About 21.00 hours on a December evening an Anson with an under training crew took off on a cross country exercise to the north of Cottesmore, the exercise was scheduled to take about three hours. I was on board to check on the work of the observer. There was no

140

moon, snow was falling and the weather forecast was worse to come.

We did fly into a few clear patches and were able to get a visual fix a couple of times. About fifty miles north of Cottesmore on our return we ran into a snow storm again at an altitude of about two and a half thousand feet. The pilot was dependent on his instruments. Some unexpected and sudden manoeuvre caused the gyros in the artificial horizon to topple. After a few hair raising aerobatics involving loss of altitude and direction the pilot regained control and the gyros settled down to normal behaviour. We regained altitude but had lost track of our position.

It was always given out at pre-flight briefings that if an aircraft was observed from the ground flying in circles the searchlights on the ground would point the way to the nearest aerodrome. Now was the time to put it to the test. Sure enough after flying a circle a searchlight came up vertical and swung over to the horizontal and after about twenty seconds was extinguished. After a further few seconds it came up vertical again and swung over to the horizontal again. We turned to fly in the direction indicated by the searchlight beam when horizontal. The next searchlight took up the task and then the next and so on until at a height of about a thousand feet we saw a night flying beacon.

From the morse code letters the beacon was flashing we knew it was the Saltby beacon. We flew over Saltby aerodrome, the officer in charge on the flare path at Saltby must have been worried about an Anson lumbering about in the dark and in a snowstorm. He would recognise the sound of the Cheetah engines. He very thoughtfully fired off two green Very lights.

We now knew exactly where we were. Those greens were much appreciated and could have been life savers. However, we were scheduled to land at Cottesmore, and this we did. It was great to be back on the ground. We were thankful to the searchlight crews, the beacon crew who kept the generator engine running on such a night and the chap who fired the greens at Saltby. The under-training crew did a good job.

So life went on at Cottesmore similar to other OTU's at the time. The sergeants mess was bursting at the seams with 'sprog' aircrew.

My situation there was that of a fish out of water. I was separated from all the Blenheim people of 1940/41, night flying on Hampdens was an alien world that I could not settle down in.

During the first week of January 1942 I had a communication from S/L SJ Monroe, my pilot on 18 Squadron at Oulton in May and June 1941. He told me he had to take a Blenheim to the Far East and that he would much appreciate it if I would go with him. He had tracked me down through Air Ministry records. As I could see no future for myself on Hampdens I agreed. Within a couple of days a signal came through posting me to Bicester.

In peace time (1920's and 1930's) when night flying training was taking place, an aerial lighthouse (also known as a landmark beacon) would be in operation on the landing ground in use. The beacon would flash the same two morse code letters every night. The code letters usually being an abbreviation of the name of the aerodrome or at least give an indication of the name. Bicester for example might flash BC, and airmen would know from their manuals that BC was Bicester.

When war broke out this procedure had to change. For each aerodrome a number of beacon sites were selected on a radius from two to five miles from the centre of the aerodrome and spaced about sixty degrees apart starting from 'site one' which would be say north of the aerodrome. Sites to be used would be selected at random, not in any sort of predictable order. To further confuse the enemy the beacon would flash a different pair of code letters every night.

So that our airmen knew where they were, before night flying each observer would be given a 'flimsy'. This was a sheet of rice paper about six inches by eight inches which listed about twenty nearby beacons, giving distance and bearing from the beacon to the aerodrome. The information was set out in a tabular form, in lines and columns. A typical arrangement of the kind of information on the 'flimsy' is shown on page 144.

If an RAF aircraft was shot down over Germany and the flimsy fell into the hands of the enemy say before 20.00 hours on a winters evening the information could be reproduced and in the hands of the pilot of an intruder over the UK before midnight. This information would enable the intruder to do a lot of damage.

To prevent this from happening, if an aircraft was considered in imminent danger the observer would eat the flimsy. Information concerning the 'colours of the day' and the 'letter of the day' were also printed on rice paper and eaten in an emergency. The 'colours of the day' were fired from a Very pistol. The 'letter of the day' flashed on the aircraft upwards and downward ident lamps or on the aldis lamp.

If an intruder fired at a beacon, the beacon and all the associated aerodrome lights would be extinguished. Any RAF airmen using the lights at the time were capable of making their own arrangements. At the first shot all lights went out, the presence of the intruder was known and night fighters would investigate.

An hour or so before dusk the aerial lighthouse, having been fitted with the appropriate cams to flash the required morse code letters, would be towed out of the aerodrome and taken to the site where it was to stand that night. The sites were at the side of hard roads, where the lighthouse could be parked on a level wide grass verge or in a field gateway, perhaps even on a village green. On a December afternoon the lighthouse would need to be flashing by about 16.00 hours and would need to be kept running until about 08.00 hours the next morning.

Where a number of aerodromes and satellites were in close proximity consultation was necessary regarding beacon sites. Beacons would need to be a reasonable distance apart. All aerodromes did not use their beacons every night.

This arrangement with the beacons remained in use with Bomber Command all through WWII.

Typical arrangement of beacon information as given on a 'flimsy' is shown below. See text on page 142.

CODE LETTERS	DISTANCE	TRUE BEARING	AERODROME
B.T.	2 MILES	180°	BICESTER
X.R.	3 MILES	270°	COTTESMORE
U.X.	2.5 MILES	053°	WATTON
M.U.	5 MILES	090°	SYWELL

The above table of information is fictitious but is typical of the information contained on a 'flimsy'.

CHAPTER TWELVE

JOURNEY TO THE EAST
MID-JANUARY TO LATE MARCH 1942

FOR LOCATION OF PLACES REFERRED TO IN THIS CHAPTER SEE MAP No. 4 (CHAPTER 5), MAP No. 5 (CHAPTER 9) AND MAPS No. 10, 11, 12 & 13.

List of illustrations etc. at the beginning of Chapter 12.

MAP No. 10.
MAP No. 11.
MAP No. 12.
MAP No. 13.

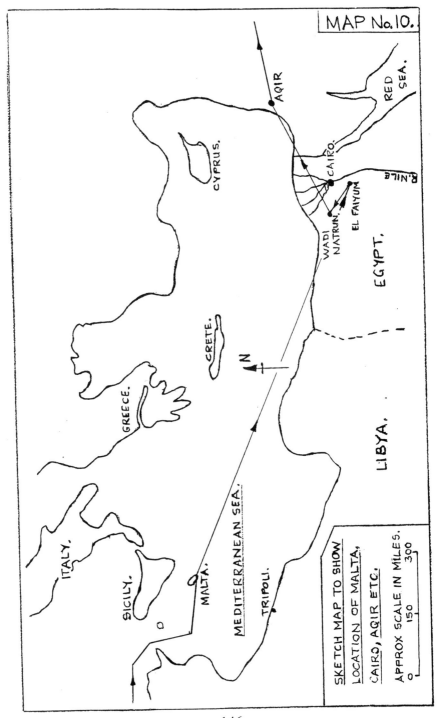

MAP No. 10.

AQIR

RED SEA.

CYPRUS.

CAIRO.

R. NILE

EL FAIYUM

WADI NATRUN.

EGYPT.

CRETE.

N

GREECE.

LIBYA.

ITALY.

SICILY.

MALTA.

MEDITERRANEAN SEA.

TRIPOLI.

SKETCH MAP TO SHOW
LOCATION OF MALTA,
CAIRO, AQIR ETC.

APPROX SCALE IN MILES.
0   150   300

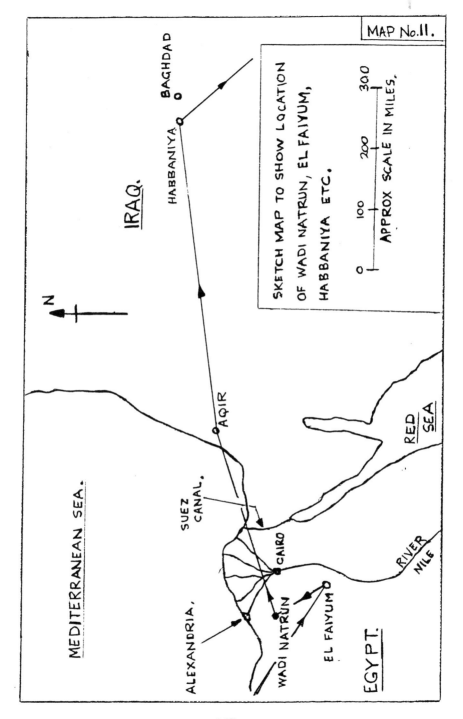

MAP No. II.

SKETCH MAP TO SHOW LOCATION OF WADI NATRUN, EL FAIYUM, HABBANIYA ETC.

APPROX SCALE IN MILES.

0   100   200   300

N

IRAQ.

BAGHDAD

HABBANIYA.

AQIR

MEDITERRANEAN SEA.

SUEZ CANAL.

ALEXANDRIA.

CAIRO

WADI NATRUN

EL FAIYUM

RIVER NILE

RED SEA

EGYPT.

147

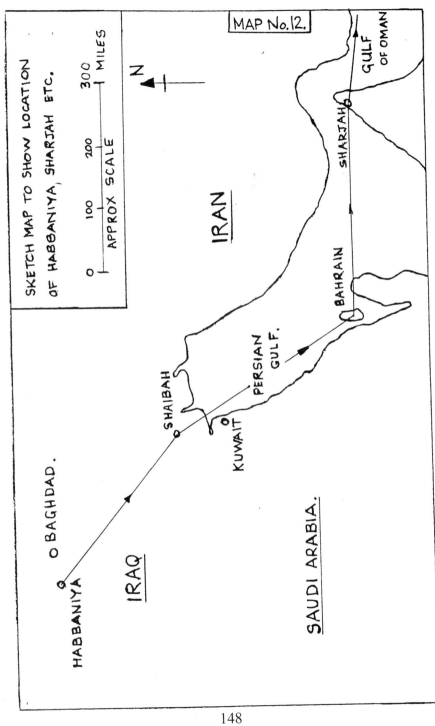

SKETCH MAP TO SHOW LOCATION OF HABBANIYA, SHARJAH ETC.

MAP No. 12.

APPROX SCALE

0   100   200   300
MILES

N

HABBANIYA

O BAGHDAD.

IRAQ

SHAIBAH

KUWAIT

PERSIAN GULF.

BAHRAIN

IRAN

SHARJAH

GULF OF OMAN

SAUDI ARABIA.

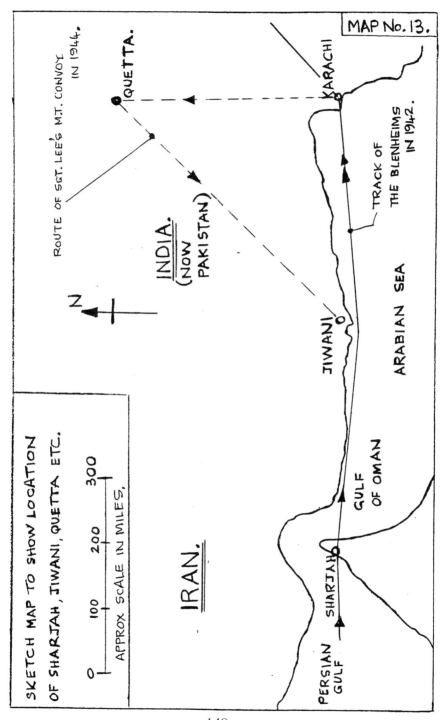

MAP No. 13.

SKETCH MAP TO SHOW LOCATION OF SHARJAH, JIWANI, QUETTA ETC.

APPROX SCALE IN MILES.

0   100   200   300

IRAN.

INDIA.
(NOW PAKISTAN)

ROUTE OF SGT. LEE's MT. CONVOY IN 1944.

QUETTA.

KARACHI

TRACK OF THE BLENHEIMS IN 1942.

ARABIAN SEA

JIWANI

GULF OF OMAN

SHARJAH

PERSIAN GULF

N

So back again to the old familiar surroundings of Bicester. The station still thronged with under-training airmen; always Blenheims on the circuit day and night, taking off and landing. As our old W.OP./AG had been taken prisoner from Malta in August 1941 we had a new one, a Sgt Eric Moss. For his story see his book 'Solvitur Ambulando' (Amberwood Publishing, Swanage, Dorset).

On February 15th we flew to Portreath in Cornwall, the departure point for aircraft going to Gibraltar and onwards. At Portreath mail bags and other gear was loaded onto the Blenheim. The aircraft number was R 3844, built by Rootes Securities Ltd. For a photograph of this aircraft see the book 'Bristol Blenheim' by Chaz Bowyer, published by Ian Allan Ltd. On Feb 16th we were off again bright and early. Again we rushed along the runway at Portreath with red hot exhaust collector rings and blue flame belching from the open exhausts. At 10,000 feet over the Bay of Biscay I began pumping up the overload petrol. After a little while petrol began to leak into the cockpit and after about ten minutes pumping petrol was squirting from the gland packing at every stroke. This was not satisfactory, we returned to Portreath.

Next day off we went again this time the hand pump for transferring the fuel worked well, and we completed the flight to Gibraltar in about seven hours. There were a number of warships in the harbour at Gib. including the aircraft carrier 'Eagle' (Ark Royal had been sunk in December 1941) and the battleship 'Malaya'. This battleship escorted every Malta convoy and survived the war unscathed. Again we had our first food on the rock in the airmen's mess. The point about this was that it ensured the officers and SNCOs knew where the airmen's mess was, what sort of food they were getting and how the other half lived generally.

The next day S/L Monroe told us we would not be going on to Malta for a week or so as he had been detailed to lead some Spitfires from 'Eagle' to Malta. We learned that 'Eagle' was carrying a squadron of Spitfires for delivery to Malta. The scheme was for a Blenheim to rendezvous with the aircraft carrier out to sea, north and east of Algiers. The fighters would be flown off and fly in company with the Blenheim to Malta. Although a Spitfire could take off from 'Eagle' it could not land on again; once airborne from the carrier the fighter had to make its own arrangements.

Hurricanes had been delivered to Malta by this means during 1941; it was whilst returning to Gib from one of these missions that Ark Royal was sunk. It was known the Germans were always watching the harbour by various means. Spain in the hands of Franco was looked on as a neutral enemy. To mislead the enemy, some days in the afternoon, we would watch 'Eagle' and her support ships sail out of Gib; next morning they would all be back in harbour.

Other days we would see all the ships safely in harbour after dark, in the morning they were all gone. Next morning they were all back in harbour. One afternoon, 6th March 1942 we were told the ships were gone and that this time it was for real. At 08.00 hours on March 7th 1942 we thundered down the runway at Gib.

We were closely followed by our 'back up' aircraft flown by a junior officer pilot. Together we set course climbing to the east. After two hours flying the hand pump for transferring the overload petrol into the main tanks was put into use. As over the Bay of Biscay it began to leak, after ten to fifteen minutes pumping, liquid petrol was squirting into the cockpit at every stroke. We could only hand over the mission to our 'back-up' and return miserably to Gibraltar.

We heard later in the day that our 'back-up' aircraft and crew had done us proud. All the Spitfires had arrived in Malta and had been up in combat that day. Next day off we went again, this time the repaired hand pump performed perfectly and after a seven and a half hour flight we landed on the besieged island of Malta. See the book 'Malta Convoy' by Shankland and Hunter, Fontana/Collins 1963. Next morning at 07.00 hours we were airborne again on a six and a half hours flight to El Faiyum, 108 MU, near Cairo and the pyramids.

At 108 MU the Blenheim R3844 was taken away from us. Before we could go on we were to wait for another aircraft to be allotted to us by Air HQ in Cairo.

For a few days we lived in a RAF approved hotel in Cairo. We saw the poverty in which many of the inhabitants lived. The streets with their deformed and mutilated beggars. The 'shoe blacks' who would throw filth onto your shoes as you walked along so that their mates could clean it off at a price. The police who would take no action unless bribed. To use 1995 words the 'culture shock' was enormous. The experience of being thrown into that environment with no warning will never be forgotten.

After those few days we moved out to a transit camp at Almaza on he outskirts of Cairo. Here we lived in tents; I seem to remember it was like the TA camps in England in the 1930s. We were only a few hundred yards from the boundary of Cairo airport and would see JU 52's landing and taking off. These aircraft would belong to the national airlines of countries that were not involved in the conflict; perhaps even Lufthansa. In the camp were airmen I had known at various places in the UK also en route to the far east.

Whilst we were at Almaza, Eric moss our W.Op./A.G.was taken ill. He reported sick and was sent to a hospital, they kept him in hospital as he was suffering from malaria. In the camp was the W.Op./A.G. who had flown out to Egypt with S/L Wells. As S/L Wells was taking up an appointment at Air HQ in Cairo his W.Op../AG was 'spare'. As we now had an aircraft allotted to us at 108 MU we needed a W.Op./AG, S/L Monroe took over Bert Warwick who was the 'spare' W.Op./AG from S/L Wells crew.

In a day or two we went again to El Faiyum (108 MU) by motor transport to pick up our aircraft. We were in company of five other Blenheim crews, we were to pick up six Blenheims and fly in company to Karachi with S/L Monroe leading. We were to take the aircraft and land at Wadi-Natrun about fifteen miles west of Cairo, from there we would set off early next morning. Late afternoon we arrived over Wadi Natrun and tried to distinguish the landing ground from the surrounding desert. This we failed to do as did four of the other pilots. After landing we realised we had landed in the desert and taxied onto the landing ground to park. The only one of the six pilots to land on the proper landing ground was P/O 'Spud' Murphy, an Australian.

The few airmen stationed at Wadi Natron lived in tents. Empty tents were provided for transit crews. In the morning we took off for Aqir in Palestine.

At that time Palestine was occupied by the British under a League of Nations Mandate. At Aqir we found an all weather runway of ample length surrounded by green countryside, the land flowing with milk and honey of Biblical times. This was a great contrast to the harsh desert of Egypt. After landing and making arrangements for the night we watched some Hurricanes doing circuits and landings, these were flown by Greek pilots.

In the morning took off again for Habbaniya in Iraq. We also occupied Iraq under League of Nations mandate. After leaving Aqir, for a time we followed an oil pipe line across the desert. At about intervals of ten miles along the pipe line was a pumping station and near each pumping station was an emergency landing ground. We did this as far as Rutbar Wells where the pipe line turned to the north east. We steered a more easterly course for Habbaniya. The aerodrome at Habbaniya was big and was a hive of activity being a RAF Aircraft Depot. Plenty of permanent buildings and hangars even a camp cinema. Due to bad weather we had to stay two or three days. During our stay we saw sand-storms such as we had been told about at school. Heavy rain falling mixed with red coloured sand blown up from the desert made it appear to be raining red mud. During our stay we attended the camp cinema and sat and ate many monkey nuts. Somehow or other I lost my field service cap. As Habbaniya was the RAF Aircraft Depot they had a vast stock of clothing so it was no trouble to get fixed up with a new cap. Some of the buildings showed scars from damage caused by Rashid Ali's artillery. The camp was only about three miles from Bagdad. It was said that Bagdad was such an evil unhealthy cesspit that it was out of bounds to British military.

After an interesting few days at Habbaniya we were away again south-eastwards making for the top of the Persian Gulf. Near Basra we overflew the RAF station at Shaibah, looked down on Kuwait and flew on out over the Persian Gulf making for Bahrain. As we approached Bahrain all was going well so we turned eastwards for Sharjah. Sharjah was an Imperial Airways landing ground and it was here that we landed. Sharjah aerodrome is situated on the western side of the neck of land that projects northwards to form the Strait of Hormuz which joins the Persian Gulf to the Gulf of Oman and the Arabian Sea. The landscape was just sand and barren rock. Imperial airways had permanent buildings there built like a fort or castle with battlements and loop holes for defence and surrounded by a large compound protected by barbed wire entanglements. A gap in the permanent entanglement allowed aircraft to be brought into the compound for protection at night. At dusk the gap was closed by barbed wire mounted on moveable structures.

The local Arabs walked about wearing traditional dress, all of them carried daggers in their belts. When airmen went to swim in the nearby sea they went in an organised party, while some bathed others mounted an armed guard. Before this was organised airmen that went to bathe did not come back and could not be accounted for.

Inside the fort Imperial Airways ran quite a luxurious hotel for their passengers. It was in this hotel that we were accommodated for the night, excellent food and individual bedrooms with 'Dunlopillo' mattresses. In the morning again six Blenheims in loose formation headed east, climbing over the rocky ridge that formed a spine for the peninsula. Across the Strait of Hormuz and follow along the south coast of Persia. Here the sea came up against sandstone cliffs two or three hundred feet high. Over the centuries soft parts of the stone have been eroded away by the weather, the sea and standstorms. This has left the harder rock standing as spires, vaulted caverns, flying buttress' and Gothic window frames. All these forms and shapes are reminiscent of the architecture of cathedrals of England, they were called by the airmen 'cathedral rocks'.

We flew over the emergency landing grounds at Jask and Jiwani and on to Karachi where there were three aerodromes: Drigh Road (the RAF aircraft depot for India), Mauripur where we landed, and Karachi Airport. At Karachi Airport we saw the mooring mast and hanger waiting the arrival of the R101 since 1930.

CHAPTER THIRTEEN

MAURIPUR, LAHORE AND 60 SQUADRON
LATE MARCH TO MID MAY 1942

*FOR LOCATION OF PLACES REFERRED TO
IN THIS CHAPTER SEE MAP No. 14.*

List of illustrations etc. at the beginning of Chapter 13.

MAP No. 14.
Aircrew at Lahore.
Frank Harbord.
Douglas "Dakota" aircraft.
Vickers "Valencia".

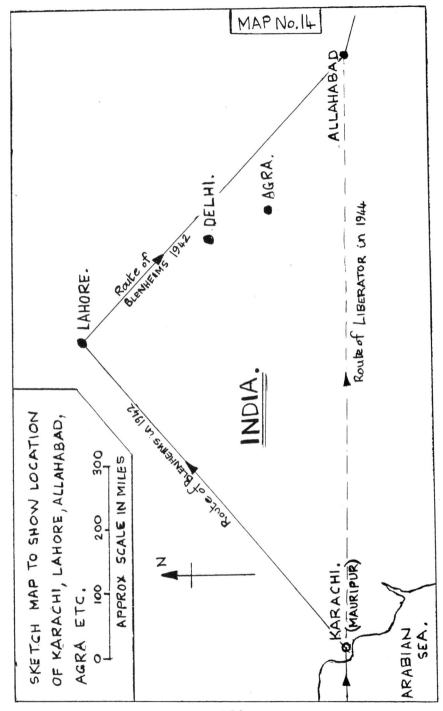

MAP No.14

SKETCH MAP TO SHOW LOCATION OF KARACHI, LAHORE, ALLAHABAD, AGRA ETC.

APPROX SCALE IN MILES

0   100   200   300

N

INDIA.

LAHORE.

DELHI.

AGRA.

ALLAHABAD.

Route of BLENHEIMS 1942

Route of Blenheims in 1942

Route of LIBERATOR in 1944

KARACHI.
(MAURIPUR)

ARABIAN SEA.

60 Squadron aircrew at Lahore, April 1942.
Photograph courtesy Sixty Squadron Archives.

Frank Harbord sitting near the entrance to one of the
sunken huts at Lahore in April 1942.

Douglas "Dakota" aircraft of the R.A.F. engaged on a supply dropping operation during W.W.2. This aircraft was known as the DC3 to the civil airlines and as the C47 to the U.S.A.A.F. Photo courtesy - M.A.P., Aslackby,Sleaford, NG34 OHG.

Vickers "Victoria" transport/troop carrier of the 1920's flying over England.
Why was the pilot so camera shy? Two Napier "Lion" engines.
This type of aircraft still in service in India in 1942.
The "Valencia" used the same airframe but with radial engines.
Photo courtesy - M.A.P., Aslackby,Sleaford, NG34 OHG.

At Mauripur we were accommodated and fed in the civil airport hotel for a few days. Officers and NCO's all in the hotel together, also with the officers and NCO's of the USAAF who had about a dozen B17's parked on the aerodrome. What the B17s were doing there and where they went I did not find out until some years later when I happened to read a book entitled 'God is my Co-pilot', by Colonel Robert L Scott. Here we first saw the smart American military uniforms. Here I met again F/S Wheaten who was 'chiefy' on 'B' flight of 82 Squadron at Watton in May 1940. He told us each B17 carried a more comprehensive tool kit than he had to maintain a whole squadron of Blenheims.

So here we were in the 'brightest jewel in queen Victoria's Crown'. Things didn't look very bright to us. It was in Karachi that we first saw the teeming, poverty stricken millions. After a few days of luxury in the airport hotel we learned we were posted to Lahore. Next morning off we all went again across the Sind desert and the Punjab. The aerodrome at Lahore had two runways, each about eight hundred yards long. The six Blenheims landed on the runway in use and parked on the hard standing near the hangars.

The aerodrome at Lahore would have been built about 1918 to accommodate aircraft such as Bristol Fighters or DH9a's. Lahore was annexed from the Sikhs in 1849 in the days of the East India Company. At the time of the mutiny 1857 to 1859 it was a garrison town. After the mutiny when the British Raj was set up the Europeans moved out of the Indian city into a Cantonment built to house the Europeans. The aerodrome was built near the Cantonment remote from the Indian city.

The city of Lahore seemed to us to be poverty stricken, the aerodrome appeared to have been built with insufficient funds. The land around seemed to be semi-desert and parched with the heat. Only the cantonement had properly constructed houses, nicely laid out gardens with green lawns. The whole place was a mystery to us. The weather was so hot that working hours for the airmen were something like 6am to 11am and then 4pm to 6pm. During the heat of the day the Europeans tried to keep still and out of the sun.

The Blenheims were to reform 60 Squadron which had been destroyed by the Japanese invasion of Malaya and Burma. 31 Squadron with Dakota's was also based at Lahore. The regular RAF people there had been there some years and were established as a garrison, they had their own married quarters and their own way of carrying on. They did not take kindly to having it all turned topsy-turvy by large numbers of transient wartime airmen.

It was at Lahore that I first heard of the title 'Provost Marshal' for the chief of the local military police. At that time I had been in the military, TA and RAF for six years. One of the old flight-sergeants who lectured us at Aldergrove advised us never to do anything that might bring us into contact with the RAF Police as they were 'unmitigated bastards'. If this description applied to corporals what could one expect from a provost marshal with the army rank of major. When the F/Sgt used the word unmitigated at Aldergrove it was a new word to me and one I have always remembered.

Because of the hot weather the barrack huts at Lahore were sunk into the ground about four and a half feet. About three feet of vertical wall stood above ground level. The walls supported a pitched roof which overhung the wall by about two feet, this overhang kept out the hot sun from the windows and kept the rain away from the walls. When standing inside and looking out of the windows your eyes were just a little above ground level.

As the mess was a distance away from the huts, as dinner time approached in the evenings the local tonga wallah's would bring their tonga's up to the huts and tout for business conveying the sergeant sahibs to the mess. Whatever clothes we wore in the daytime we were required to be properly dressed in the mess in the evening, long khaki drill slacks, with khaki drill tunic and black tie or khaki drill bush shirt. When one walked back from the mess to the hut the sky was like black velvet studded with bright twinkling stars, all around were twinkling fireflies and the air filled with the croaking of frogs. Frogs also jumped about on the floor of the hut. One evening a chap arrived back at the darkened and empty hut. He went down the steps and before switching on the light he threw onto the concrete floor a very short stub of a lighted cigarette (smoking was encouraged in those days, and no filter tips).

When he switched on the light he was aghast to see a frog in great trouble where he had thrown the cigarette stub. The frog apparently mistaking the lighted stub for a firefly had swallowed it without hesitation. The frog died. At Lahore, you could arrange for the 'nappy wallah' to shave you whilst you were still in bed and before reveille. An experienced nappy wallah moved about so quietly and had such a gentle touch you could be shaved without being woken up.

After a few days at Lahore we were told that we were now on the strength of 60 Squadron. Sixty was an old India squadron. It had moved to Singapore to meet the Jap invasion of Malaya and had been annihilated; most of the flying crews had been lost in action. Aircraft on the ground had been destroyed by enemy action. Probably less than a dozen aircrew from the old squadron got back to Lahore. Some had walked over the hills from Burma into India.

My pilot, S/L Monroe DFC, was promoted Wing Commander and was appointed to command the new 60. His two flight commanders were S/L Webster DFC and bar and S/L Cawdery. S/L Webster had won his DFC flying a Hampden with Bomber Command over the Channel ports in the winter of 1940/41. S/L Cawdery was an old India hand. His face still bore the scars of injuries suffered a few years earlier, in the biplane days. Engine failure necessitated an emergency landing, during which his face came into contact with the instrument panel.

The squadron started a training programme. Cross-countries, local formation flying, night flying circuits and landings, bombing practice on the ranges at Peshawar. For the practice bombing we moved up to Rawalpindi for a few days, say two aircraft at a time. There was no black-out at Lahore. One of the pilots on a dark night at Lahore was given landing clearance and told the direction of the runway. He was making his final approach and was down to about three hundred feet when he realized the lights he had taken to be the runway lights were in fact the lights along the long platform of Lahore railway station. He opened the throttles slowly to full power, clawed for altitude, up undercarriage and flaps, trim the mixture control, propeller pitch, throttles, adjust the elevator trim and begin the landing

163

procedure again, this time on the proper runway lights.

Another evening when walking from the mess to the huts, with Bert Warwick, about 22.00 hours, we heard the rising roar of a Blenheim's engines on take off. Suddenly silence and stillness, just the twinkling of the stars and the fireflies and the croaking of the frogs. Then the sound of rending and tearing metal from the aerodrome boundary. We both began running towards the sound. There we saw the wreckage of the Blenheim. The W.Op/AG was out of the kite and staggering about, dazed. We looked in the open hatch above the pilots cockpit, the pilot and observer were sitting in their seats apparently OK. They began to struggle up out of the kite, then sat on the ground shocked and bruised. The ambulance arrived and took the crew to the sick bay. The pilot was the same Australian P/O Spud Murphy who was the only one of six to land inside the aerodrome boundary at Wadi Natrun.

So the training programme went on. About every two weeks I flew with W/C Monroe to Delhi to report to Air HQ. Returning to Lahore on one of these trips a 31 Squadron Dakota drifted past us, obviously making his way to Lahore. The W/C took up a position on the starboard side of the Dakota and flew in formation with it. We were disappointed to find that the cruising speed of the Dakota, a civil airliner, was a few mph faster than the Blenheim, a front line fighter/bomber. While we were at Lahore on a couple of occasions a Vickers 'Valentia' landed and took off. These aircraft were large biplanes, two engines, that the RAF were still using for communications, they were of wooden construction and were developed from the 'Vimy'. The wingspan would be about a hundred feet and they would carry about twenty soldiers.

The C/O's aircraft at Lahore was Z7495. The ground crew decorated this aircraft with a picture of the devil, with cloven hooves, horns and a pitch fork. Below the picture in a scroll they wrote the words 'The Old Man Himself'. The picture was on the side of the aircraft near the nose.

In the middle of May 1942 it was considered the squadron was fit for operations. We flew in 'The Old Man Himself' from Lahore to Asansol, refuelling at Allahabad.

CHAPTER FOURTEEN

ASANSOL AND 60 SQUADRON
MID-MAY TO MID-DECEMBER 1942

FOR LOCATION OF PLACES REFERREDTO IN THIS CHAPTER SEE MAP No. 15 & MAP No. 16 (CHAPTER 16).

List of illustrations etc. at the beginning of Chapter 14.

MAP No. 15.
S/L Monroe War Grave record.
S/L Monroe citation.
60 Sqdn. Blenheim.
Blenheim and bomb trolley.
Blenheim and Bill Fallon.

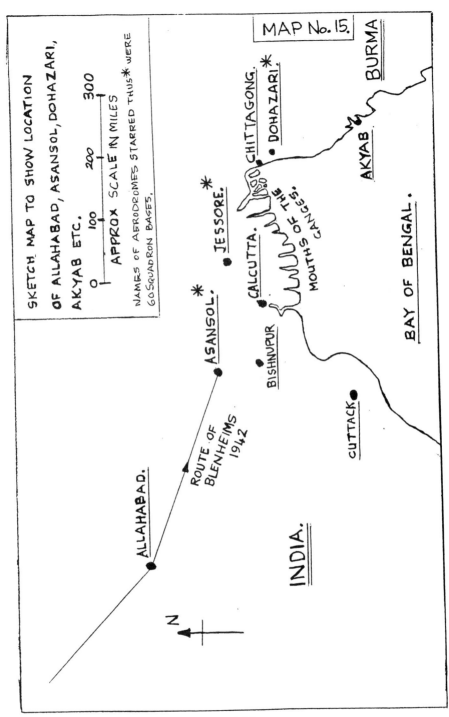

MAP No. 15.

SKETCH MAP TO SHOW LOCATION OF ALLAHABAD, ASANSOL, DOHAZARI, AKYAB ETC.

APPROX SCALE IN MILES

0   100   200   300

NAMES OF AERODROMES STARRED THUS* WERE 60 SQUADRON BASES.

ALLAHABAD.

ROUTE OF BLENHEIMS 1942

ASANSOL.*

BISHNUPUR

CALCUTTA.

JESSORE.*

CHITTAGONG.

DOHAZARI*

MOUTHS OF THE GANGES.

BURMA

AKYAB

BAY OF BENGAL.

CUTTACK

INDIA.

N

166

Commonwealth War Graves Commission

2 MARLOW ROAD MAIDENHEAD BERKS SL6 7DX
Telephone 01628 34221 Telex 847526 Comgra G Facsimile 01628 771208

Further to your enquiry we record the following:

Casualty:	Sqdn. Ldr Pilot SYDNEY JOHN MONROE, 37685
Awards:	D F C
Served With:	Royal Air Force
Died:	29/10/1942
Commemorated:	KHARTOUM WAR CEMETERY
	Sudan
	Plot 6. Row E. Grave 10.
Additional Information:	Son of Harold and Belle Monroe; husband of Violet Madeline Monroe, of Morden, Surrey.

Khartoum is the capital of the Sudan. The War Cemetery lies on the south-eastern side of the town adjoining the Khartoum New Christian Cemetery.

Courtesy Commonwealth War Graves Commission.

A.M. BULLETIN NO. 3611

19th April 1941.

ROYAL AIR FORCE AWARDS NO.198.

The King has been graciously pleased to approve the following awards in recognition of gallantry displayed in flying operations against the enemy:-

Awarded the Distinguished Flying Cross.

Flight Lieutenant Sidney John MONROE No.82 Squadron.   In April, 1941, this officer was detailed to carry out an attack on enemy shipping off the Frisian Islands.   In spite of bad visibility he succeeded in locating a 3,000 tons ship escorted by flak ships.   In spite of accurate fire from the flak ships, he scored direct hits from a low level and the ship was last seen down by the stern.

During this attack a shell burst in the cockpit, killing the observer and wounding Flight Lieutenant Monroe in the ankle.   In spite of this wound, he brought his aircraft safely back to base.

This officer has displayed great gallantry and devotion to duty and has at all times shown determination in pressing home his attacks.

60 Squadron Blenheim IV, Asansol, December 1942. Standing with hands in pockets and wearing a topee is S/L. WEBSTER D.F.C. and bar.

Photo courtesy Sixty Squadron Archives

60 Squadron Blenheim Mk.IV and trolleys of 250 pound bombs at Asansol 1942. Photo courtesy Sixty Squadron Archives.

Blenheim Mk.IV of 60 Squadron, squadron code letters 'M U' aircraft letter 'Y' aircraft number Z5883. This aircraft was loaned to 113 Squadron for an operation and landed at Charbutia in the condition shown in the photograph. The pilot, on the strength of 113 Sqdn. was Bill Fallon, January 1943. (Reproduced with the kind permission of Comm Squadron Aviation Photos.).

The aerodrome at Asansol had an all weather runway about seven hundred years long, but in the process of being extended. Asansol was a small town, it was a coal mining district and had railway yards and workshops. It is about a hundred and twenty miles west of Calcutta.

Why the runway was there I don't know, there had been no RAF station there. To accommodate the airmen a camp had been built by local contractors. The walls of the buildings were of wattle and daub type of construction. The roof trusses made of local rough hewn green timber on which were laid pantiles of local manufacture. All very primitive but superior to anything the local population lived in. The weather was very hot, one day it was said to be 128 degrees Fahrenheit in the shade. When the monsoon rains came these huts stood up very well.

The flying crews were a mixture of Australians, New Zealanders, Canadians etc, only about 25% from the UK. As well as being hot the weather was very humid, this caused 'prickly heat' an irritating and unsightly rash on the skin. Chaps also began to suffer from heat exhaustion, dysentery, even malaria. Chaps would be taken to hospital, often that was the last we saw of them. (By the time they came out, we had moved on or their places on the squadron had been filled by others and the originals were posted elsewhere.) As the Japs had captured all the quinine we began to take mapacrine tablets, one a day, to prevent malaria. We also swallowed salt tablets to replace the salt lost in perspiration.

In a large country house about two miles from our camp lived the manager of the local coal mine. Every day he would be driven through the camp by his Indian chauffeur in his big luxurious American car. He had a swimming pool in his gardens, he invited us to go to his house and use his pool as nobody else used it. From conversations we learned he was a Scot from Glasgow. He had been in India in the coal mining business for twenty three years and had no desire or intention of returning to the UK. While we swam in his pool in the evenings he would sit on his verandah with his 'burra peg'. When we had had enough he would call his chauffeur and we would be taken back to camp in his car.

He was interested in conditions in the camp. All the time water was being pumped out of his coal mine and allowed to drain away. At his own initiative and expense he piped some of this water towards our camp. On the opposite side of the road, not more than twenty to thirty yards away from the huts he set up a bath house. When I say he did it, of course he did not do it with his own hands, he arranged for his engineers and staff to do it. Where the water reached the shack he had built it was raised up to a height of seven or eight feet. Running the length of the shack and down the middle he fixed up a cast iron pipe about four inches in diameter and with the end blanked off.

The pipe was about fifty feet long and at intervals of about four feet holes about half an inch in diameter were drilled horizontally across and through the pipe. When the pipe was filled with water at a pressure the water issued from the holes almost horizontally at first then falling in a cascade to the ground. They had somehow arranged a concrete floor and a means of drainage. Duckboards were provided for the bathers to stand on. The pumping out of the water from the mine went on twenty four hours a day, so as a by-product of the coal mine the airmen enjoyed cool sparkling showers at any time of day.

This was the time of Gandhi and his 'civil disobedience' campaign. Wherever we went we were greeted by the words 'Quit India' painted up on all the walls and wherever else they could put it. We had gone there to save them from the horrors of a Japanese occupation; being told to 'Quit India' was not encouraging. The domestic camp had its normal guard room, in addition other guard posts had been set up on approaches to the camp in about half a dozen places, each post manned by a couple of chaps. Each outpost was connected by telephone to the main guard room.

Every day about a half dozen flying crew that were not required for flying would be detailed to spend the day in the guard room as a back up to the outposts. If called on the phone we would jump into the lorry provided and be driven to where we were needed. We had a variety of weapons including two Thompson sub-machine guns. These tommy guns were the genuine article with the circular ammunition drum as used by Al Capone in the St Valentine's Day Massacre.

On our bombing and gunnery course at Aldergrove we had learned to dismantle, clean, oil and reassemble various machine guns, the Lewis, Browning, Vickers GO etc. While on stand-by in the guard room at Asansol to pass the time away we dismantled, examined and reassembled the Thompson sub machine gun. Some months later while on a ground defence course up in the hills, during a lecture on the Thompson gun we were told that on no account should certain parts be dismantled except by specialists.

In fact our services were never called for at Asansol, we did answer practice calls to prove that the system worked. Round about the camp were trees say about forty feet high. Some kind of monkeys lived in these trees. The monkeys looked on us as interlopers and took no notice of our attempts to shoo them away when they came walking about the camp. One day they went into the hut and came out with a chaps wallet. The monkey took it up onto the roof and sat on the ridge tiles, at leisure it took out and examined the papers, tore them up or crumpled them up and discarded them. Some of it was money, ten or fifty 'chip' notes (a rupee was always called a 'chip' by the airmen). The owner could only stand and watch and fret. When the wallet was empty it too was just discarded on the roof and the monkey ambled off to join his companions.

Another form of wild life that caused trouble were the kite hawks. They were always watching for any kind of foodstuff. To us they seemed to behave like dive bombers. One day an unsuspecting chap set out from the sergeants mess kitchen to carry a plate full of potato chips to his mates. A flock of kite hawks began 'dive bombing' the plate. They did not collide with each other nor did they touch any part of the chap carrying the plate or the plate itself. By the time he got to the hut the plate was empty.

About mid June the SW Monsoon broke. Strong gusty winds, ten-tenths of low clouds, torrential rain, thunderstorms etc. Ghandi and his civil disobedience campaigners were still on the go. They went about setting fire to letter boxes and pulling up railway lines. To prevent trains being derailed Blenheims patrolled the lines, any suspicious activity being signalled back. To disperse a crown interfering with the railway line the Blenheim would dive low over their heads and fire Very lights. During these operations Blenheims did go missing due to accidents. Patrolling the railway could go on for four hours, these operations were known as 'internal security patrols'. On one of these patrols one of our kites came back with about five and a half feet missing from one wing tip due to collision with a signal gantry.

All the ground that had been baked as hard as concrete now began to soften, the 'paddy fields' were flooded. It was now important that aircraft taxied on the hard taxi tracks and motor vehicles used the hard roads. During the dry weather the Chance Light had been parked on the hard baked earth near the watch office. When it was required for night flying a tractor with big pneumatic tyres went to tow it to where it was needed, the tractor became bogged down. A big four wheel drive Thorneycroft lorry attempted to pull out the tractor but that too became bogged down. Bring on an American ten wheeled Studebaker with a winch at the front. With no trouble he hauled out the Thorneycroft, then the tractor then the Chance Light.

About mid-July, without warning W/C Monroe was posted to Khartoum and his place as O/C 60 Squadron was taken over by W/C Wallis DSO. Within weeks of leaving Asansol W/C Monroe was dead, killed while flying a Hurricane at Khartoum. This sudden posting and death was a blow to me from which I have not yet recovered. Myself and Bert Warwick now had no pilot, we found ourselves on a squadron where English chaps were in a minority, the majority being Australian, Canadian and New Zealanders. At least we still had the same two English flight commanders. All these 'Empire' airmen displayed their country of origin by means of shoulder flashes proclaiming 'Canada', 'Australia' etc. One of our English pilots had some shoulder flashes made for himself on which he had embroidered 'England Thank God'. This initiative was not approved of by the authorities.

On May 12th 1942, due to shortage of serviceable aircraft, Warrant Officer Boyd was detailed to fly 'The Old Man Himself' on operations. On his take off run when he was going about seventy miles per hour, one of his engines cut, the kite swung off the runway and collided with a pile of hardcore or some such material that was being used on the runway extension. No one was hurt although the kite was extensively damaged. One day in June Bert Warwick and myself were on the aerodrome, whatever we had been doing I can't remember. I can remember we were exhausted and jaded. We went to the watch office where they were brewing tea, they offered tea to us but had no cups. They did have empty condensed milk tins that had been opened by crude army type tin openers leaving sharp rough edges. From these tins we drank the tea and I still remember it as the best tea I have ever tasted, it was a real elixir of life.

Within thirty six hours of taking over 60, W/C Wallis called all aircrew to a lecture in the marquee that we were using as a crew room. He spoke about his past experience in the RAF and with the Mk I Blenheims of 45 Squadron in Abyssinia, using eight hundred yard runways. Although he was due for repatriation, he was staying on with 60 Squadron as he had plans, hopes and ambitious for the Squadron. Unbeknown to any of us in that marquee on that day, the Gods also had plans which they were saying nothing about.

A fortnight after this lecture W/C Wallis took off to attend a funeral in Calcutta. He landed at Dum Dum where the runway was being extended in a similar manner to that at Asansol. Whilst taxying to his parking place W/C Wallis taxied off the taxi track and onto the soft ground. The Blenheim sank into the soft earth to such a depth that the propeller blades were striking the ground. The crew left the aircraft and reported to the maintenance organisation to get the aircraft dug out and repaired.

It was not easy in July 1942 to lay hands on a spare serviceable Blenheim propeller at short notice. By working through the night the engineering section at Dum Dum hoped to have the kite serviceable by seven o'clock the next morning. The next morning, early, the wing commander took the aircraft and with his own crew on board plus a south African pilot and another W.Op/AG of 60 Squadron who needed a left back to Asansol, taxied out to the end of the runway. He turned into wind and opened the throttles for his take off run. As with Warrant Officer Boyd at Asansol one of the Wing Commanders engines cut dead, this swung him off his line of take-off and he crashed headlong into a group of heavy vehicles and material required for the work on the runway extension. The W/C and two others were killed instantly, the two others on board were seriously injured and were not seen on the squadron again.

The Squadron was stunned by this event. S/L Cawdery, the senior S/L took over command of the squadron. Operations continued as before. Eric Cawdery filled the post of C/O for some months and in his own quiet conscientious manner restored some stability and confidence to the squadron.

About a fortnight after the death of W/C Wallis, Bert Warwick and myself were sent to Lower Topa for a ground defence course. Lower Topa was a hill station at an altitude of about seven thousand feet in the foot hills of the Himalaya Mountains. It was near the town of Murree on the road to Kashmir. We travelled by train to either Rawalpindi or Peshawar, from the railway station to the camp was about forty miles by road. Being airmen we were conveyed these forty uphill miles by motor transport. (Army chaps marched these forty miles, they must have had an overnight camp en-route).The temperature in the hills was like England in the summer and the whole place more civilised.

We did our ground defence course and travelled back to rejoin the squadron. So things went on with Eric Cawdery as C/O. The road through Asansol was called a 'grand trunk road'. It joined Calcutta with such places as Cawnpore, Lucknow and Delhi. Despite its title the road was just a strip of tarmac ten to twelve feet wide with a 'soft shoulder' of unmade up road on either side, these soft shoulders were also about ten to twelve feet wide. The only motor vehicles seen to use the road were military vehicles, the local bullock wagons and pedestrians used the soft shoulders in the dry weather.

It was along this road that the army of the East India Company had marched in 1857/58 to the relief of the besieged Europeans in Lucknow and Cawnpore. They marched at night to avoid the worst of the heat. We used to go and look at a grave yard where they had buried their dead at the side of the road. This graveyard containing say twenty five graves was in 1942 overgrown and uncared for, even then a relic of a dead empire of only about eighty five years ago. In Asansol itself there was a proper British Military Cemetary and this would be properly maintained. I would presume it is now looked after by the War Graves Commission.

When the monsoon broke and water gathered the frog population was multiplied and water snakes appeared all over the place. These snakes were harmless and did their best to avoid men. If accidentally kicked or trodden on they would bite. The local Indians walking about with bare feet were at a disadvantage. The coal mine manager's swimming pool now became infested with water snakes and frogs and could not be used. He advised us to carry a torch light and a bamboo cane at night, any snake that came within striking distance could be disabled by a smart blow across its body.

It was said that eighty per cent of snakes in India were harmless, people that were bitten died of shock. We did fear the Cobras although we never saw one in the wild. About this time on a couple of occasions an American P40 painted with the sharks teeth appeared over the aerodrome and landed on the runway. From reading the book 'God is my Co-Pilot' this must have been flown by Colonel Robert L Scott himself as he tells us that he was flying the only one that existed in that area at the time.

The bullock carts and ox-wagons that plodded along the 'Grand Trunk Road' were very primitive. Having only two wheels they needed no steering gear. At the speed they travelled and having wheels about five feet in diameter they needed no suspension. The ox-wagons pulled by two oxen had the animals harnessed on either side of a central pole. At night a hurricane lamp was hung from the forward extension of this pole and the oxen plodded on while the driver was having a sleep in the back.

Getting into a Blenheim that had been standing in the hot sun was an unpleasant experience. Wearing only shirt and shorts this clothing became drenched in perspiration, things improved a little when the engines started, creating a draft of air.

The hand holds on the control column, the throttle levers etc were too hot to be touched by bare hands. Gloves had to be worn to protect the hands. To reach our targets in the Irawaddy valley we had to climb to ten thousand feet to get over the hills, where the cold set the teeth chattering and made concentration very difficult. This was a problem that was never solved. Flying from Asansol we would use Dum Dum, Agartala, Chittagong or Fenny for advanced landing grounds as necessary.

Airmen flying in India in the days of open cockpits had devised a 'flying topee'. This was a flying helmet similar in style to the leather helmets we wore but made of a porous and lightweight woven fabric with a flap at the back to protect the back of the neck. The crown of the head being protected by a reduced size narrow brimmed imitation of a normal topee. This helmet was cooler, gave ample protection from the sun and carried the earphones and microphone needed for the intercom. As well as targets in the Irrawaddy valley we attacked, at low level, ships, docks and airfield at Akyab, installations on Oyster and Ramree Islands.

Sharing the aerodrome with us at Asansol was 113 Squadron, also with Mk IV Blenheims and commanded by W/C Walter. Conditions at Asansol at that time were confused, not to say chaotic. Survival was the best we could hope for. We just hung on and hoped things would improve. Compared to the treatment being meted out to the chaps who had been captured by the Japs we lived a life of luxury.

Asansol was surrounded by terraced paddy fields. The boundary of the fields was marked by clay walls about a foot high and eighteen inches wide. These walls were also used as footpaths to enable people to walk around and between the fields. Where the ground was undulating the rain water would be retained in the fields by the low clay boundary walls so that the whole area was flooded and stood in water. When the farmers of the fields on the higher levels decided their ground had had enough water they would break a notch in the surrounding wall so that the water would flow to a lower level. The water would flow through a basket-work fish trap. They would catch in this trap sufficient fish to make the effort worthwhile. The fish would be four to five inches long. I have never heard a satisfactory explanation as to how the fish got there, as in the dry weather the fields would be baked like concrete.

Towards the end of August the monsoon began to fade away and by mid September the monsoon was over. The high humidity was gone, with daytime temperatures in the eighties things seemed comparatively pleasant. S/L Cawdery was still acting CO, running things in his own quiet unassuming manner. He was complemented and supported by S/L Webster. On the outside S/L Webster was swashbuckling, jaunty and with a cavalry mans panache. Behind this facade S/L Webster was thoughtful and thorough. He did what he had to do with a flourish, he would never ask anybody to do anything that he hadn't done himself and which he was not prepared and willing to do himself again. All the squadrons officers were of the best.

It had been expected that when the monsoon ended the Japanese would attack into India across the 'sundabunds', the Ganges delta. To frustrate this expected invasion we did exercises with the army in the area. The attack did not happen.

CHAPTER FIFTEEN

JESSORE AND 60 SQUADRON
MID-DECEMBER 1942 TO
LATE JANUARY 1943

*FOR LOCATION OF PLACES REFERRED
TO IN THIS CHAPTER SEE MAP No 15 (CHAPTER 14)*

At the end of November/beginning of December 1942 the squadron moved to a new aerodrome at Jessore. The new aerodrome was a magnificent two thousand yards long concrete runway with taxi tracks and hard standing etc. From the air it could be seen from twenty miles away. The squadron aircraft were flown to the new landing ground, no trouble. The NCO aircrew were billeted in stone built houses in the small town of Jessore. The houses had been taken over for the purpose, what had happened to the original inhabitants I don't know. An extra large house was taken over as the sergeants mess.

The rest of the squadron personnel and all the squadron equipment were transported on a special train. Along the route the train caught fire, the squadron equipment and railway trucks were extensively damaged, but no casualties. This fire was the subject of an enquiry that went on for months and resolved nothing.

At Asansol and at Jessore we slept on 'charpoys'. These were locally made beds and were just a wooden frame work with morticed joints. Many yards of stout webbing were then wrapped across the framework to make a horizontal surface, the webbing then being wrapped from end to end and woven into the cross ways loops, this made a reasonably comfortable bed. These beds were always infested with bed bugs. The bed bugs were reddish brown colour, about 0.15 inches long by 0.1 inches wide, oval in shape. They were about 0.02 inches thick.

The size and shape of these bugs made it easy for them to crowd into the gaps in the loose fitting mortice joints in the woodwork and the interstices where the webbing crossed over. A party of Indians had a full time job of going around all the billets with a sheet metal bath big enough to dunk a charpoy in. In the bath was a liquid something like paraffin that got rid of the bugs for a week or so. The bugs didn't trouble me but some chaps just could not sleep.

Where the officers' mess was I don't know. S/L Cawdery did come round to satisfy himself all was well. It was about this time a new CO was appointed. He was Wing Commander Banks, a Canadian from Newfoundland. He took over so unobtrusively that it was a week or more before we realised he was there. He was a chap who carried on in a similar manner to S/L Cawdery, he gradually gained the confidence of the squadron.

Things went on as routine. Christmas Day came and we had a parade in the morning and a march past the new CO. Warrant Officer. 'Paddy' Huggard was the senior warrant officer on the squadron and was therefore Chairman of the Mess Committee (sergeants mess). At lunch time the CO and some other officers were entertained by Paddy Huggard in his capacity as CMC in the sergeants mess.

The squadron went on flying operations as ordered. About this time the authorities began issuing a ration of cigarettes. These cigarettes were specially made for the military with the brand name of 'V for Victory'. To those of us who did not smoke they were a joke. I remember chaps somehow joining three cigarettes together in the shape of a letter Y. By placing the single end in the lips and putting a match to the other two ends two 'Victory' cigarettes could be smoked at the same time. These double barrelled cigarettes they called 'Y for Yorker'. Serious smokers complained loudly about the quality of the Victory cigarettes. After a few weeks they were replaced by cigarettes with a known brand name such as 'Players'.

The old Royal Flying Corps song:
> 'Betrayed by the country that bore us,
> Betrayed by the country we find,
> The best men have all gone before us,
> And only the dull left behind.
> So raise your glasses steady,
> So raise your glasses high,
> Here's a toast to the dead already,
> And here's to the next man to die.'

was sung in the mess with much feeling. Towards the end of January 1943 the squadron was on the move. This time again to a new aerodrome known as Dohazari, about twenty miles south of Chittagong.

While at Jessore, for reasons now forgotten, the aircrews on occasions would 'bomb up' their own aircraft. This only applied when 250lb bombs were being carried. The bombs would be delivered to the aircraft by the usual tractor drawn train. The observer would get down on his hands and knees underneath the bomb rack, with his head towards the aircraft nose. The pilot and air gunner would then lift the bomb onto the observer's back. Using leg, arm and back muscles the observer would then raise the bomb up towards its rack.

The bomb would be guided at the nose and tail by the pilot and air gunner until the lug on the bomb engaged on the electro-magnetic hook on the bomb rack. Once engaged the bomb could only be released by applying an electric current to the solenoid. As soon as the 'clunk' was heard of the hook engaging the lug, all could relax. The bomb steadies were then adjusted and the arming device engaged.

The bomb was still safe as the safety device was still held in place by the safety pin. Just before take off the observer removed the safety pin from the bomb. When over enemy territory the pilot would operate the bomb arming switch.

The striker in the nose of the bomb was protected by a domed cover screwed onto the bomb. This cover had wind vanes around its outer periphery. While this cover was in place nothing could touch the striker, therefore the bomb was safe. The cover was prevented from being unscrewed by the arming fork. If the bomb was dropped 'safe' it would fall away from the aircraft with the arming fork in place, the striker was protected and therefore the bomb would not explode.

If the bomb was dropped 'armed' the arming fork was pulled out of the bomb and retained on the bomb rack. The slip-stream would impinge on the wind vanes on the domed cover over the striker, it would unscrew from the bomb and fall away leaving the striker exposed. There was now no way of stopping the bomb from exploding.

While we were at Jessore the Japs began night bombing of Calcutta. This caused great panic and alarm amongst the Indians in Calcutta, they began to flee from the city in large numbers. However we now had based in the Calcutta area a detachment of 89 Squadron with night fighter Beaufighters. One night one of these Beaufighters intercepted a formation of three Jap bombers flying in formation with navigation lights on. The Japs did not see the Beaufigher. The pilot, F/O Crombie RAAF manoeuvred the Beaufighter into a suitable position and then gave the Japs the benefit of his four twenty mm cannons. All three Japs were destroyed. A few days later Flight Sergeant Pring from the same squadron detachment gave a repeat performance. These two incidents coupled with the shooting down of odd Jap bombers in the district made the Japanese decide to call an abrupt halt to the bombing of Calcutta.

CHAPTER SIXTEEN

DOHAZARI AND 60 SQUADRON
LATE-JANUARY TO LATE-MAY 1943

FOR LOCATION OF PLACES REFERRED TO IN THIS CHAPTER SEE MAPS No. 15 (CHAPTER 14) & No. 16

List of illustrations etc at the beginning of Chapter 16.

Map No. 16.
F/O "Micky " Duncan.
60 Squadron's Blenheim IV's attack Akyab.

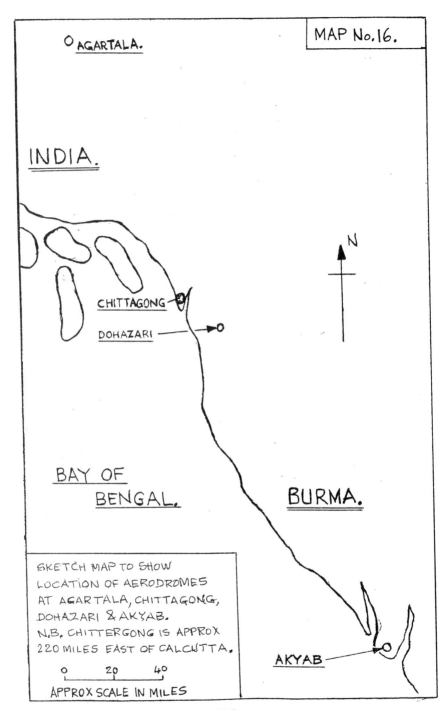

O AGARTALA.

INDIA.

CHITTAGONG

DOHAZARI

N

BAY OF
BENGAL.

BURMA.

SKETCH MAP TO SHOW
LOCATION OF AERODROMES
AT AGARTALA, CHITTAGONG,
DOHAZARI & AKYAB.
N.B. CHITTERGONG IS APPROX
220 MILES EAST OF CALCUTTA.

0   20   40

APPROX SCALE IN MILES

AKYAB

F/O. " Mickey " Duncan, Dohazari, 1943 .
He is wearing official R.A.F. issue sun glasses.
These sun glasses were distortion - free and could be worn
by a pilot during take - off and landing .
Photo courtesy Sixty Squadron Archives

60 Squadron's Blenheim IV's attack Akyab, summer 1942.
Photo courtesy Sixty Squadron Archives.

The aerodrome at Dohazari was a two thousand yard runway of sun baked earth where the paddy fields had been levelled. The taxi tracks and dispersals were of similar material. Where the aircraft were parked blast walls had been built to protect the aircraft. These blast walls were about six to eight feet high arranged along three sides of a rectangle big enough for the Blenheim to be pushed in from the fourth side. Thus the aircraft was protected from three sides, the fourth side being a risk we had to take.

To get material to build these walls, pits had been dug into the ground behind the three blast walls. These pits were about six feet square and dug about five feet deep leaving a walkway at the original ground level about two feet wide between each pit. I imagined this was done such that the ground could be restored to its original level when the blast walls were no longer needed. The blast walls were just loose earth piled up so that the sides sloped about forty five degrees, the natural angle of repose for loose earth. To get sufficient material it will be realised the pits covered an area of over thirty feet away from the walls. The buildings on the aerodrome, flight offices, stores etc were all built of bamboo.

The domestic camp was about a mile from the landing strip and built in amongst trees. All the domestic buildings were also of bamboo. No nails or screws were used in these structures, all the joints being made by binding or lashing the elements together with cord like vegetation obtained from the local jungle as the bamboo itself was. Some of the binding material was long and very thin slivers of bamboo, the bindings being drawn very tight and knotted by workmen who used both hands and their bare feet.

Dohazari was the end of the railway line that came down from Chittagong. In anticipation of the army making an attack into Burma large amounts of stores came down and were unloaded from the railway, from then on stores had to be transported by road. To make a hard surface for the roads rough bricks were made locally. When laid on a prepared surface these bricks appeared to make a good road surface.

Around the railway station many shops and cafes sprang up offering goods and services to the passing military personnel. It was here I first saw limes and drank natural lime juice cordial.

The squadron bombed enemy aerodromes and installations in the Irrawaddy Valley but much of the effort was now in support of the army which had begun a limited push down the Arakan coast and the Mayu Peninsular with the objective of capturing the island of Akyab with its port and all weather aerodrome before the onset of the monsoon in June.

When the army called for air support we would fly to the position given. As we approached at a height of one thousand feet the army would fire smoke bombs from mortars into the Japanese positions. We would then drop our bombs onto where the smoke bombs were bursting. From a height of one thousand feet we could hear our bombs exploding. From army reports the Japanese didn't like this. Down with the army at the front line we now had RAF officers acting as advisers and liaison officers. Doing this liaison job at one time was W/C Nicolson, the only Battle of Britain VC. He came into the officers mess at Dohazari one evening and talked to the squadron officers. He confirmed the effectiveness of these operations and gave it as his opinion that the Japs would not allow us to get away with it much longer. W/C Nicolson VC, DFC, was killed on 2nd May 1945 flying in a Liberator of 355 Squadron which crashed into the sea, south of Calcutta.

One day flying with F/L Morphet and returning to Dohazari we were at a height of about six thousand feet over the Mayu peninsular and about twenty miles north of Akyab, flying in the usual box of six. Casually looking down through the triplex panel I saw green wings carrying red discs darting about. The red disc, the Japanese national marking, showed up much better than I had expected. They came up nearer so that they could be positively identified as Army Oscars.

The Oscars began making attacks on the Blenheims from the rear. The twelve Brownings from the Blenheim turrets gave them a hot reception. As well as the twelve Brownings in the turrets they also had to dodge the twelve Brownings fired from under the nose by the Observers. The Oscar pilots were not in the mood that day to die for the Emperor. After a number of attacks they did succeed in doing some damage to the kite immediately behind us. This kite being flown by an Australian, F/O Archer, with his Australian observer and Bert Warwick as W.Op/AG. When F/O Archer had to fall out of the formation the Oscars decided they had had enough for that day.

F/O Archer realised he was in trouble with an engine out and flying controls damaged, he decided he could not get home. He shouted for his crew to jump. The observer jumped, Bert Warwick clipped on his parachute, opened the top hatch and tried to get out. However he found the violent manoeuvres of the aircraft and the 'g' forces prevented him from getting out. F/O Archer was hanging on trying to control the aircraft such that Bert could jump. When they were down to about eight hundred feet Bert called his pilot and said "I've had it, I can't get out, you jump".

Reluctantly Archer jumped. There now being no restraining hand on the control column the aircraft went into some violent manoeuvre in the opposite direction and Bert found himself flung out of the aircraft. He pulled his rip-cord and floated gently down in his parachute. He told me when he arrived back at Dohazari that when he landed and was gathering up his chute he shouted repeatedly, "I'm alive, I'm alive." In those few minutes he had made up his mind to die, the relief at finding himself on the ground and unharmed caused him to shout to the world that he was still alive.

At times when nothing was going on we would spend time improving and renovating the slit trench that we would use as a shelter in the event of a raid by Japanese bombers. Each hut had its own trench. We made steps for entrance and exit. We placed across the top bamboo poles one and a half to three inches in diameter and on the top of the bamboo piled earth about a foot thick. The Japs did come with their bombers. Near the aerodrome we had a battery of heavy ack-ack, four point five inch calibre from memory. We also had on the aerodrome perimeter anti-aircraft machine gun pits.

When the ack-ack were notified Jap bombers were coming in our direction they would fire a single round to explode at the expected height of the bombers, this was our air raid warning. When we were in the domestic camp and we heard this single shot we would scan the sky for the bombers, there were usually about fifteen and being airmen ourselves we knew from the position of the formation and the direction they were going where they intended to drop their bombs. Usually it was the aerodrome that was the target. We had no need to take cover as we were a mile away; we would watch and see what happened.

The ack-ack would put up a barrage, the kites would drone on and release their bombs. The bombs would burst on or in the vicinity of the runway. As the kites went out of range the barrage would die away and quiet would return. We would all then go to the aerodrome, and starting at one end of the runway and spreading out all across the width of the runway we would walk its full length looking for and picking up any bits of shrapnel that we saw.

We had learned to do this by experience as Blenheims had been damaged on take-off and landing due to tyres being punctured by shrapnel. One day we heard the single warning shot and leisurely inspected the sky. As soon as we saw the formation we knew that the domestic camp was the target. We all piled into the slit trench. We crouched in the trench listening to the barrage and the swish and bang of the bombs. The vibration caused a host of red ants to fall from the roof of our shelter onto the bare heads, chests and backs of the chaps in the shelter.

The camp had been showered by light anti-personnel bombs so damage was not severe. One of the Australians had hung his blue overcoat up on a coat hanger with the back of the coat against the bamboo wall of the hut. When we came into the hut it still hung there with its buttons shining. He was aghast when he took it down to find the back all ripped out by shrapnel. The Japs bombed the aerodrome about once a week, but only on that one occasion did they come to the domestic camp.

One afternoon we were briefed for the next morning. We were to be in the ops room by 08.30 hours to stand by go give support to the army when they called for it. We were to be escorted by a squadron of Mohawks who would fly in at about 07.30 hours, re-fuel and stand by with us. Next morning about 07.00 hours racing aero engines and machine gun fire could be heard from the direction of the aerodrome and this went on for about five minutes. I knew at once what was going on but most of the chaps could not be bothered to get out of bed.

A squadron of 'Oscars' had got over the aerodrome at tree top height undetected by the radar and spent a lively five minutes shooting up the Blenheims. The Oscars departed having had not a shot fired at them. At 07.30 the squadron of Mohawks that were to stand by with us appeared over the aerodrome and the ground defences opened up with everything they had. The squadron leader of the Mohawks made off as fast as he could and came back ten minutes later, this time to land without incident. He was very put out about the reception he got on his first approach. The Mohawk was a similar airframe to the P40 Tomahawk but had a radial engine. Needless to say no Ops that day, just inquests.

We began to hear stories about a Japanese reconnaissance aircraft that was over Dohazari, Chittagong and other aerodromes taking photographs every day. The aircraft was a 'Dinah' and it would fly over at twenty five thousand feet where the Hurricanes could not close with him. The aircraft became known as 'photo Johnny' and he had a radio tuned to the frequency of the Hurricanes, on which he would jeer at the Hurricanes inability to get up to him. He didn't know it, but there was a surprise in store for him. The RAF obtained a Spitfire of a suitable mark that had the capability of dealing with the Dinah. They smuggled it into Chittagong and kept it and nurtured it where 'photo Johnny' didn't see it. One day when he was looking down at the Hurricane trying to get up to him and giving out his usual contemptuous remarks in his perfect English he received a blast from the Spitfire he hadn't seen.

The next day another Dinah went the same way and then a third. As with the night bombing of Calcutta, the Japs looked for a different game to play. The RAF played another trick on the Japs. A whole squadron of Spitfires arrived secretly at Chittagong at the same time as a squadron of Royal Navy ships bombarded Ramree Island. Out came the Jap bombers with their escort of Oscars and flew into something they didn't expect. The Japs never got near the ships, only a few stragglers from the Jap formation limped home. The Spitfires roared back to Chittagong without loss.

On one occasion, flying with W/C Banks, we took off for an operation when engine trouble appeared immediately after take off. W/C Banks jettisoned the bomb load 'safe' and switched on the jettison for the outer fuel tanks, he was able to make a circuit and land on the runway. A search party had to go out to search for and recover the bombs.

When an aircraft took off at Dohazari a great cloud of dust was blown up. After the first aircraft took off the next one had to wait until the dust cloud cleared such that he could see his way clear down the runway. One day Sgt. Hardman was sixth to take off and was determined to get off as quick as he could to join the formation. For this reason he opened his throttles heading where he estimated the runway was, although he couldn't see for the dust cloud. In fact he was about twenty to thirty degrees off and when going at about seventy mph he ran onto an area near one of the dispersal pens where earth had been excavated as detailed early in this chapter.

The undercarriage dropped into the first holes and the nose structure, back to the leading edge of the wing was torn off as the aircraft continued to move forward on its belly. The observer who was sitting beside the pilot and had not put on his lap belt fell out into the next hole and the aircraft slid on over the top of him. The aircraft came to rest against the blast wall with Sgt. Hardman's knees gently embedded in the soft earth. He was able to walk away from the wreckage, his observer Sgt Ivan Olaf Gilbert was able to scramble up out of the pit with cuts and bruises and also walk away. The W.Op/AG was shaken, cut and bruised.

All three were taken to hospital at Chittagong. Sgt. Hardman came back the same day, the other two were kept in for a few days. In fact the squadron moved before they were discharged from hospital and they didn't rejoin the squadron. The observer was born in India. One of his parents was Russian, the other Swedish, hence his Christian names of Ivan Olaf.

Another day, about dusk much activity broke out in the camp. An RAF reconnaissance aircraft had spotted twenty four Jap bomber aircraft newly parked on an airfield in the Irrawaddy valley. Our twelve Blenheim's were bombed up and all preparations made for take off at first light to catch the Japs still on the ground and bomb them. As soon as there was enough light to see the runway we were off the ground and heading for the target.

When we arrived over the jap aerodrome not an aeroplane was to be seen on the ground. We turned for home leaving the Jap runway pock marked with bomb craters. On arrival over our runway at Dohazari we saw the reason there were no Jap aircraft on their aerodrome. Our runway was also covered with bomb craters. We all managed to get down unharmed as I expect the Japs did.

About this time I was attending various interviews etc in respect of being promoted to commissioned rank. I had also been recommended for pilot training and travelled to Air HQ in Delhi for the medical. That was the reason I was in Delhi the day Earl Wavell had his 'coronation' parade on his appointment as Viceroy of India. My promotion to the rank of Pilot Officer came through in September 1943 and notification that I would shortly receive instructions regarding attending pilot training school.

Back to Dohazari. For one of the interviews I flew to Chittagong in a Blenheim piloted by Sgt Schragger, a South African. The time now was the beginning of May 1943 and the army push was stopped about ten miles from the southern tip of the Mayu peninsula. To get onto Akyab island landing craft were needed. The story was that the landing craft had set out from England but that they had been purloined by the middle-east for the invasion of Sicily.

There was fear all round of the monsoon starting early and everything becoming bogged down. The Japanese resistance in the Mayu peninsula was stiffening. In view of the circumstances it was decided to abandon the attempt to capture Akyab island and the army began to pull back. In the third week of May 60 Squadron left Dohazari and flew via Alipore (Calcutta) - Vizagapatam (refuelled) to Yelahanka, about five miles north of Bangalore in southern India.

CHAPTER SEVENTEEN

YELAHANKA, St THOMAS MOUNT AND 60 SQUADRON
LATE-MAY TO END OF AUGUST 1943

FOR LOCATION OF PLACES REFERRED TO IN THIS CHAPTER SEE MAP 17.

List of illustrations etc. at the beginning of Chapter seventeen.

Map No. 17.
Frank Harbord citation .
Frank Harbord Warrant.

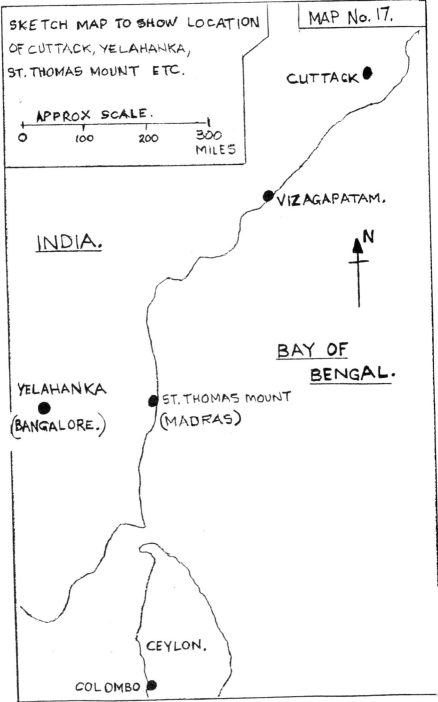

SKETCH MAP TO SHOW LOCATION
OF CUTTACK, YELAHANKA,
ST. THOMAS MOUNT ETC.

MAP No. 17.

APPROX SCALE.

0   100   200   300
                  MILES

CUTTACK

VIZAGAPATAM.

INDIA.

N

BAY OF
BENGAL.

YELAHANKA
(BANGALORE.)

ST. THOMAS MOUNT
(MADRAS)

CEYLON.

COLOMBO

198

URGENT NEWS.

A.M. BULLETIN NO. 10777, Serial 622.

ROYAL AIR FORCE AWARDS NO.606

The KING has been graciously pleased to approve the following awards in recognition of gallantry and devotion to duty in the execution of air operations:-

Distinguished Flying Medal.

581215 Flight Sergeant Frank Alfred Harbord, No.60 Squadron.

Flight Sergeant Harbord has flown on a very large number of operations against enemy targets in Europe, the Middle East and Burma. On many of these flights he has served as leading navigator/ bomb aimer. At all times he has performed his duties with exceptional coolness and devotion to duty, contributing in no small measure to the many successes achieved.

WARRANT

The Right Honourable the SECRETARY OF STATE FOR AIR

To   Frank Alfred Harbord

By virtue of the Authority to me, by the King's Most Excellent Majesty in this behalf given.
I do hereby Constitute and Appoint you to be a Warrant Officer in His Majesty's

Royal Air Force   from the   First

day of February   1942 , and to continue in the said Office during the pleasure of the
Right Honourable the Secretary of State for Air.   You are therefore carefully and diligently to
discharge your Duty as such by doing and performing all manner of things thereunto belonging, as
required by the Established Regulations of the Service, and you are to observe and follow such Orders
and Directions as you shall receive from your Commanding, or any other, your superior Officer,
according to the Rules and Discipline of War.

GIVEN under my Hand and Seal of the Air Council this   Third
day of March 1942

200

The aerodrome at Yelahanka was a new one with a two thousand yard concrete runway at an elevation of about three thousand feet. Due to the elevation the climate was more pleasant than east Bengal/ northern Burma. We felt we had left the war behind at least until after the monsoon. The runway at Yelahanka had its ups and downs. The watch office had been built in one of the 'downs' such that the ends of the runway could not be seen from the watch office. While we were there a new one was built on one of the 'ups' and this was satisfactory.

By this time I had received promotion to Warrant Officer. The promotion was dated February 1942, this is an indication of the state of communications between London and India in those years. I was now flying regularly with W/C Banks. S/L Cawdery had gone from the squadron and had been replaced by S/L Lindsell. We did much training at Yelahanka, the weather always seemed to be good. We gave demonstrations of bombing to all sorts of army commanders. We took part in mock battles with other units. In some of these battles I was one of the umpires, a position I enjoyed. Bombing competitions were organised in which I took part flying with W/C Banks.

One afternoon I was notified that W/C Banks wanted to see me in the Officers Mess at 18.00 hours to discuss a bombing competition in which we were taking part. As I approached the mess at the appointed time I was met on the steps by W/C Banks and shepherded inside where most of the other officers were assembled. He told me there was nothing to discuss, it was just a ploy as he wanted to be the first to congratulate me as he had been notified of the award of the DFM to me. After a couple of sherrys, congratulations and hand shakes from all the officers I went back to the sergeants mess to satisfy their curiosity as to what it was all about.

Sid Schragger, with whom I had flown from Dahazari to Chittagong a few weeks before, was killed with his observer F/S Brister a couple of days later, due to engine failure. He had no W.Op/ AG with him that day as he was only doing local flying. They were buried in the local military cemetery, all the flying crews attended and shots (blanks) were fired over their graves. While we were at Yelahanka both W/O (Paddy) Huggard and myself had the blue barathea warrant officers uniforms made by a military tailor in Bangalore (I still have the tunic).

At Yelahanka the weather forecast was received in special code. I was sent on a course for a few days to learn to decode the signals. Seven o'clock every morning I was in the crew room sweating over decoding the met signals. At first this used to take me three quarters of an hour, as the weeks went by I became more proficient and could do it in about ten minutes. As I decoded the signals people came to look on me as the met expert. For a practice operation the squadron was involved in, the briefing was to be carried out as for a real operation. As I de-coded the met signal the CO asked me to chat about the weather. The briefing was attended by the Maharajah of Mysore. (Yelahanka is in Mysore state). The Maharajah was suitably impressed.

After being at Yelahanka for about eight weeks, about the end of July 1943, the squadron moved again to St Thomas Mount. St Thomas Mount was an aerodrome about two miles north of Madras. This aerodrome was at sea-level so it was back to the extremely hot humid weather similar to Bengal. Within a few days of moving we learned that the days of 60 as a Blenheim squadron were numbered.

Flying with W/C Banks one day we were approaching to land at St Thomas Mount. When at a height of about three hundred feet, there was a clunk and the aileron controls went stiff. To keep the wings horizontal took all his strength. When safely on the ground we found that just outboard of the propeller arc on the port wing the leading edge had been knocked back about six inches over a length of about a foot. From the blood and feathers around the dent it was obvious we had hit a vulture. The tubular metal linkage that operates the ailerons on the Blenheim runs inside the wing leading edge, it was bent and fouled up by the damage.

The squadron was to re-equip with Hurricanes. All observers and air gunner wireless operators would be posted. All pilots over the age of twenty six were considered too old to fly Hurricanes, they would also be posted. The squadron would be taken over by the young S/L 'Dickie' Lindsell. So old comrades began to drift away in ones to other squadrons, mostly to Dakota squadrons that were then growing. Bert Warwick, who had flown with W/C Monroe and myself from the middle East to Lahore to re-form 60 Squadron in March 1942 was posted to 31 Squadron. That was the last I saw of him.

Bert's family lived in Raunds in Northamptonshire. In the 1970's I looked for him in the phone book but without success. I looked for him at Burma Star reunions, also without success. I tried to contact him through the 31 Squadron Association, from them I learned to my dismay that Bert, his wife and young family had emigrated to Canada in the 1960s and that Bert had died there. So in Canada now there must be some young Canadians who have a hazy idea that in the dim past they had a grandad Warwick who was a World War II airman.

Crest of No. 60 Squadron, Royal Air Force.

Translation of motto, "I strive through difficulties to the skies".

The crest depicts the head and horns of a Kabuli Markhor, a mountain goat found in the vicinity of the Khyber Pass.

Illustration and information courtesy of 60 Squadron Archives.

CHAPTER EIGHTEEN

FLYING CONTROL, MAURIPUR
AND JIWANI
END OF AUGUST 1943 TO END OF MAY 1944

*FOR LOCATION OF PLACES REFERRED TO IN THIS CHAPTER
SEE MAP No. 13 (CHAPTER 12) & MAP No. 1*

List of illustrations etc. at the beginning of Chapter 18.

Map No. 18.
Map No. 19.
Commissioning parchment.
"Empire" flying boat.
Vickers "Vildebeest".
Armstrong - Whitworth "Ensign".

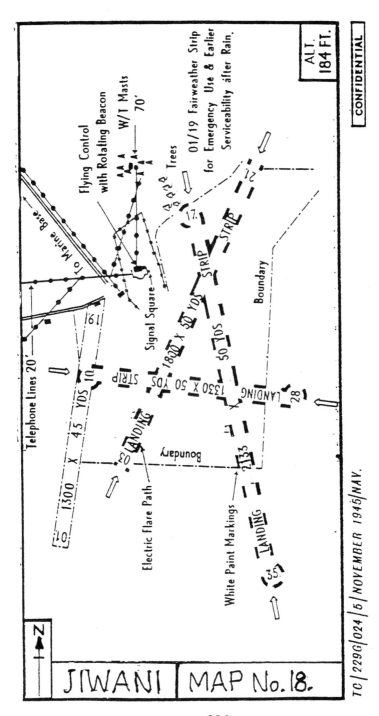

Map content labels:

ALT. 184 FT.

CONFIDENTIAL

Flying Control with Rotating Beacon

W/T Masts 70'

01/19 Fairweather Strip for Emergency Use & Earlier Serviceability after Rain.

Trees

To Marine Base

17

STRIP

STRIP

Signal Square

Boundary

1800 X 50 YDS

50 YDS

21

Telephone Lines 20'

1300 X 45 YDS

10

STRIP

1330 X 50 YDS

LANDING

28

03

LANDING

Boundary

Electric Flare Path

White Paint Markings

21

33

35

LANDING

N

JIWANI MAP No. 18.

TC/229G/024/5/NOVEMBER 1945/NAV.

Reproduced with the kind permission of Comm Squadron Aviation Photos.

206

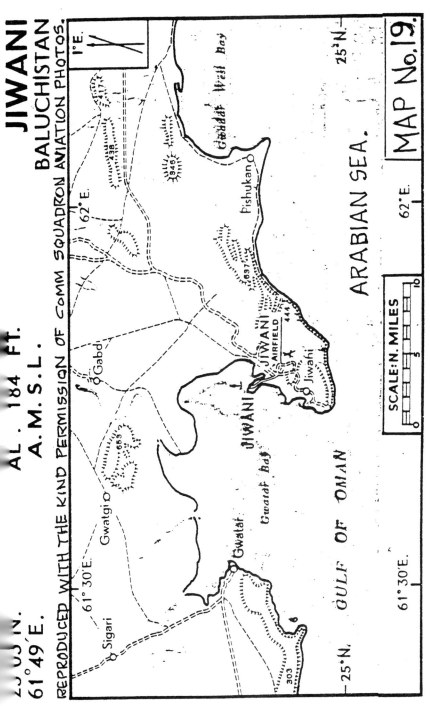

Reproduced with the kind permission of Comm Squadron Aviation Photos.

George **R.I.**

George VI, *by the Grace of God,* OF GREAT BRITAIN, IRELAND AND THE BRITISH DOMINIONS BEYOND THE SEAS, KING, DEFENDER OF THE FAITH, EMPEROR OF INDIA, *&c.*

To Our Trusty and well beloved **Frank Alfred Harbord** Greeting:

WE, reposing especial Trust and Confidence in your Loyalty, Courage, and good Conduct, do by these Presents Constitute and Appoint you to be an Officer in Our *Royal Air Force* from the *Eleventh* day of *June* 1943. You are therefore carefully and diligently to discharge your Duty as such in the Rank of *Pilot Officer* or in such higher Rank as We may from time to time hereafter be pleased to promote or appoint you to and you are at all times to exercise and well discipline in their Duties both the inferior Officers and Airmen serving under you and use your best endeavours to keep them in good Order and Discipline. And We do hereby Command them to Obey you as their superior Officer and you to observe and follow such Orders and Directions as from time to time you shall receive from Us, or any your superior Officer, according to the Rules and Discipline of War, in pursuance of the Trust hereby reposed in you.

GIVEN at Our Court, at Saint James's the *Twenty first* day of *September* 1943 in the *Seventh* Year of Our Reign

By His Majesty's Command

Short's Ltd. "Empire" class flying boat of Imperial Airways as used in W.W.2. In this photograph the aircraft has been taken out of the water and is mounted on a set of temporary wheeled trollies .

PHOTO COURTESY - M.A.P., ASLACKBY, SLEAFORD, NG34 OHG.

Vickers Ltd. "Vildebeest". The aircraft flown at Jiwani had no cowling around the engine and was fitted with a two bladed wooden propeller.

PHOTO COURTESY - M.A.P., ASLACKBY, SLEAFORD, NG34 OHG.

Armstrong Whitworth "Ensign" of Imperial Airways. These aircraft were first introduced in 1937 and frequently passed through Jiwani in 1943/44.

PHOTO COURTESY - M.A.P., ASLACKBY, SLEAFORD, NG34 OHG.

About the end of August 1943 I was posted to a Flying Control course at Mauripur, where we had first landed in India in march 1942; where we had seen Colonel Scott and his B17s. I set off by myself on the long railway journey from Madras to Karachi. From memory it took five or six days and involved a number of changes of train. I have hazy memories of spending a day or more on the Nagpur state railway which was narrow gauge, less than three feet.

The Flying Control course lasted a month. It was run by a W/C, his deputy was a S/L Saul. S/L Saul was looked on with great respect as he had been co-pilot with Charles Kingsford-Smith on some of his epic record breaking flights in the 1930s. The lecturers were full of enthusiasm having had experience on Bomber Command aerodromes in the UK and believing that as soon as Germany was finished with there would be such a flood of aircraft from the UK to South East Asia that we would be overwhelmed. About twenty chaps were on the course, about half of them were flying airmen, the others had been selected from various non-flying appointments.

At the end of the course I was posted to Jiwani in Buluchistan. Jiwani was about three miles east of the Iranian border and a mile inland from the sea. The country side was just rugged desert. The landing ground was a two thousand yard long strip of hard sand, free of rocks. About two miles from the aerodrome was the Imperial Airways flying boat station. Two or three times a week and Imperial Airways 'Empire' flying boat would alight at their flying boat base.

In between flying-boat movements Imperial Airways 'Ensign' four engined passenger aircraft would land on the aerodrome. The Imperial Airways signals system was excellent, their manager at Jiwani knew exactly when an aircraft would be landing. They had a building on the aerodrome not far from the watch office. When an 'Ensign' landed the Imperial Airways station manager and his staff would be waiting and would escort the passengers from the aircraft to their building which they used as a refreshment centre, assembly point, office, waiting lounge etc. After the 'Ensign' took off all Imperial Airways personnel would disappear back to their flying boat station. There was always the closest co-operation between Imperial Airways and the RAF. As well as the flying boats and the 'Ensigns', Imperial

Airways also used a small number of 'Lockheed 12' twin engine airliners.

The CO of the RAF station was Major Bodley of the South African air force. He was a pilot and what we would now call a colourful character. He was six feet tall, athletic, outgoing, jolly, little respect for authority, friendly, not particularly military. He was always where he was needed using local resources to do whatever was required. Like the Earl of Bandon and W/C Monroe he would talk on equal terms to the 'erks' and was looked on with affection by all.

As well as Major Bodley the station had a strength of about a dozen officers. These were the station adjutant, MO, Signals Officer, Engineering Officer, Flying Control Officer (myself), two Indian Air Force Officers who ran the Met Office, a Captain Johnson of the Royal Engineers, and various others that I cannot now call to mind. The strength of the sergeants mess was about the same. In all, from memory, I estimate the total strength at about a hundred.

The RAF station took its name from a nearby village. Some of the locals made a living by fishing from boats, how all the others managed to keep body and soul together I don't know. There always seemed to be plenty of Indians, the women always carrying babies and living in poverty.

As well as the RAF and Imperial Airways, Jiwani was home to a flight of Po2's of the Russian Air Force and a team of civilian scientists headed by a Russian professor. This organisation was engaged in the study and elimination of locusts. Swarms of locusts flew across this area of desert in their search for food. The locusts settled on the ground at night and could not fly on again until the sun was up and gave sufficient heat to dry the dew off their wings.

As well as the Po2's, the flight had a Royal Air Force 'Anson' which had been fitted up with tanks containing insecticide and spraying equipment. Every morning before dawn the Po2's were out on reconnaissance looking for swarms of locusts grounded by the dew. When a swarm was found a signal was sent giving the position and the Anson would take off and that swarm of locusts would be eliminated.

Standing near the watch office was a Vickers 'Vildebeest'. This was one of a squadron that had passed through some months before. It had gone u/s and had been left behind and forgotten about. In spare

213

moments the airmen examined it, and using much time, ingenuity, patience etc they were able to get the engine running. The 'Vildebeest' was a large single engine biplane torpedo bomber. From the manufacturers name plate it was seen this particular one was built in 1936. The Vildebeest had been superceded by the 'Swordfish'.

After doing further work and examining the airframe minutely the airmen felt sufficiently confident to ask Major Bodley to give it some taxying trials. The major agreed. The engine was started and he carefully taxied around the landing strip. All appeared to go well and he turned to taxi across the aerodrome. To our surprise the Vildebeest became airborne, climbed to a thousand feet, made a couple of circuits of the aerodrome, landed and taxied back and parked near the watch office where it had started from.

When he stepped down from the Vildebeest the major said he had not set out to take off. He was doing a high speed taxying run across the aerodrome, examining his instruments, oil pressure, brake pressure etc. When he looked up over the side of the cockpit he was amazed to see he was airborne and climbing.

In the next few weeks the major flew the Vildebeest most days. Confidence in the aircraft now was such that the major applied to the Group Captain at Mauripur for authority to keep the aircraft at Jiwani to be used for communication flights. The Group Captain agreed and asked the major to fly the aircraft to Drigh Road where it would be given a thorough check over. So Major Bodley flew the Vildebeest to Drigh Road.

After a couple of weeks he contacted Drigh Road to enquire how the overhaul of the Vildebeest was progressing. He and the whole station were shattered to learn the reply was that as the type was obsolete it had been dismantled and struck off charge.

The 'entomological flight' was commanded by a Russian air force major and he had about twenty Russian air force personnel under his command, pilots and ground crews. They lived in their own barrack block and remained aloof from their British counterparts. Bread and other rations for all ranks were supplied by the British. All the bread for the camp was baked on the camp by the British in their cookhouse. At one time the cookhouse ran out of bread making ingredients. Supplies were not expected for three days, so for that time emergency rations would be issued in lieu, (hard tack or ships biscuits). This was accepted by the British airmen.

The Russian major came over, somewhat crestfallen, to say his chaps were giving him a hard time regarding no bread. They had pointed out to him that Stalin had promised them bread not ships biscuits and could we do anything to help him out. Signals flew between Jiwani and Karachi and it was arranged and agreed that a Po2 would fly to Karachi and bring back as much bread as could be stowed on board. This flight was carried out and tranquility was restored. Living on 'hard tack' was not seen as a great hardship by the British.

The main reason for the aerodrome being at Jiwani as far as the RAF was concerned was to refuel reinforcement aircraft flying through to India, and this was going on all the time. Beaufighters, Mosquitos, Blenheim MkVs, Barracudas and Hurricanes were our main customers. The Hurricanes came through in batches of twelve at a time. On one occasion eleven Hurricane's landed although twelve had taken off from Sharjah. None of the pilots had seen anything, 'request news' signals to Sharjah and Jask produced no results. All the Hurricanes were refuelled, nine went on to Karachi and two flew back along the route they had flown before but nothing was seen. It was a great relief next morning about 09.00 hours to receive a signal from an Imperial Airways flying boat to say he had spotted a Hurricane down in the desert twenty miles west of Jiwani and a mile north of the coast.

Again Imperial Airways came to the rescue. They had a rescue launch and this was loaned willingly to the RAF with its experienced crew. A search party with rations and water set off along the coast, landed in an appropriate place, went ashore and inland and found the Hurricane. The pilot was a Greek. After take off from Sharjah his wireless had gone dead. About fifty miles west of Jiwani his engine had begun to fail. He could not call anybody and he could not keep up with the formation. He gradually lost height until he had to make a wheels up landing in the desert.

When he realised he had to spend the night out in the desert he 'ripped' his parachute to make himself a shelter. No doubt it was the white silk of the parachute that attracted the flying boat captain's attention. The Hurricane pilot was greatly relieved to be rescued.

There was no direct road from Jiwani to Karachi. Motor vehicles had to be driven from Karachi to Quetta. Quetta is about three hundred miles north of Karachi. In 1935 Quetta was devastated by a severe earthquake. After Quetta the vehicles had to be driven another three hundred miles over desert roads in a south westerly direction to reach Jiwani. About the end of March 1944 there was a change of command at Jiwani, Major Bodley was posted away and S/L Speedy took over as CO.

Since October 1943 I had been Flying Control Officer at Jiwani and now by April 1944 there was much American activity in the area. Over the past months they had flown in much building material and had built huts as the beginning of a domestic camp. They continued to fly in building material and put up more and bigger buildings. They were entirely self supporting, independent of the British altogether. They arranged their own rations. They did not accept RAF met forecasts or RAF signals. They set up their own signals station and their own met office. One of the C47's came in one day laden with building material, bags of cement, breeze blocks, a petrol driven cement mixer and a piano!

All rations and stores came to Jiwani by air. The RAF had an arrangement with Indian National Airways that they flew into Jiwani with their DC2s weekly. Personnel needing to travel to and/or from Karachi would get on the INA if convenient. Other than that chaps would make their own arrangements with the pilots of any RAF aircraft that was going in the right direction at the right time and had some spare room.

We received a signal from Karachi that they had seven or eight MT vehicles there that were allotted to Jiwani and that we were required to collect them. Our MT sergeant (Sgt Lee) was given the job of making all arrangements. He had done the trip before and knew all the difficulties. A few weeks before this a Hurricane from one of the convoys had gone u/s at Jiwani. Spares had been sent up by INA from Karachi and the Hurricane was now serviceable.

Off went Sgt Lee and his dozen MT drivers by various aircraft to Karachi. Next day off went S/L Speedy in the Hurricane. He was to attend various meetings and then go on a fortnights leave. As I was then the senior GD officer on the statinon I became acting CO and station routine orders were issued under my name. The engineering officer was a F/O Stallibrass, he had ideas of going out into the desert to recover the damaged Hurricane. He assembled tackle he thought he might need and with a couple of volunteers from the engineering staff he went off with a two ton Bedford truck. His idea was to get the kite up on its wheels, remove various awkward bits and get the tail up onto the back of the lorry such that he could tow it home.

At Karachi Sgt Lee appraised the vehicles that were to comprise his convoy, he arranged water containers, spare petrol and oil and other gear to cope with emergencies. Five days after he had left Jiwani a signal was received from Quetta to tell us the MT convoy had left, making for Jiwani. As dusk approached the convoy had not arrived. After dark, standing on the watch office roof, lights could be seen twinkling in the direction of the road and it was presumed these must be the headlights of the convoy. When first seen these lights must have been ten to fifteen miles away. For over an hour the lights were watched as they grew brighter and eventually the convoy rolled triumphantly into the station and parked in the MT yard.

All the drivers were exhausted and it was obvious Sgt Lee was in a bad way. He was taken into the sick bay by the MO (F/O Gilbert-Fraser) and put to bed there. Next morning at about 11.00 hours the MO came to me and said he was extremely worried about Sgt Lee. The MO was unable to make any diagnosis or bring about any improvement, it was his opinion that Sgt Lee should be got into hospital as soon as possible. I therefore sent off a signal 'immediate' priority to Karachi asking for an air ambulance. No reply came to this signal.

About 15.00 hours the INA DC2 supply flight landed and amongst the passengers was a corporal medical orderly. He said he had been sent in reply to our signal to assist our MO. Naturally our MO was aghast at this snub from Karachi. About 16.30 hours an American C47 landed and parked near the watch office. It was flown by an American Lieutenant and was another load of building material which he said they would unload in the morning. About 18.00 hours the MO came to me again and said Sgt Lee's condition was deteriorating and he must be got to hospital.

I went across to the American mess, found the pilot of the C47, told him the situation and asked him if he would fly Sgt Lee to hospital. He was very willing to do this if we could get his kite unloaded. The entire strength of the RAF station descended on the C47 and had it unloaded and ready for flight in about half an hour. It was now about seven o'clock in the evening and dark. While the C47 was being unloaded Flying Control had laid out and lit a 'goose neck' flarepath. At Jiwani we still used the old pre-war paraffin goose neck flares for night flying.

Soon after 7 o'clock that evening the C47 thundered off the runway and disappeared in the blackness in the direction of Karachi. On board was the American crew, Sgt Lee on a stretcher and two medical orderlies. At the expected time we received the 'arrival' signal from Karachi. Then all settled into an uneasy calm. About 15.00 hours the next day amongst the other signals traffic came a signal to say that Sgt Lee had died in hospital. No cause of death was given, nor was the cause ever given. Our MO was concerned, was it infectious? Were any of the other MT drivers on that convoy threatened? It seemed to us that the authorities at Karachi were not particularly interested in their satellite at Jiwani. I don't remember any senior officer ever coming on a tour of inspection, nor do I remember any padre ever paying a visit.

F/O Stallibrass was out in the desert with his assistants working on the damaged Hurricane. There being no other means of contacting him a 'runner' was organised. He went off carrying a written signal from me telling him what had happened to Sgt Lee and that they were to abandon the Hurricane and return to camp. By the time they received my signal they had the Hurricane up on its wheels. They reluctantly picked up their gear and all returned to camp. Whatever it was that killed Sgt Lee never affected anybody else. In the approximately eight months that I was at Jiwani I don't recall anybody else having to be kept in the sick quarters or sent to hospital at Karachi.

In my time no serious accidents occurred on the aerodrome. A Mk V Blenheim overshot the landing ground and was wrecked. A Beaufighter's undercarriage collapsed. One of Imperial Airways Lockheed 12s had one undercarriage leg collapse. A tail wheel tyre burst on a Mosquito. These were just incidents, no one was injured. Imperial Airways repaired their Lockheed 12 themselves and it flew away.

At the appointed time S/L Speedy came back and my short glory days as acting CO came to an end. Soon after that, one day there was extremely bad weather at Karachi. It got so bad that they closed the aerodrome and all aircraft flying between Sharjah and Karachi that were making for Karachi were diverted to Jiwani. So we had a great fly-in that day, mostly American. We had half a dozen C47s, three RAF Dakotas, a half a dozen American twin engine light bombers with tricycle undercarriages, type name or numbers now completely forgotten. The weather at Jiwani was good but the great mass of black cloud could be seen to the east.

The RAF Dakotas were carrying an ENSA concert party and amongst them were the stars of British radio, Elsie and Doris Waters and 'Stainless Stephen'. They volunteered to give a show that evening. The airman's mess was converted to a theatre. The Imperial Airways station manager was invited up to attend as he had kindly offered accommodation for some of the people. He came up in his big American Cheverolet station wagon, a real cross country vehicle. For this great influx of people beds and food had to be found, this responsibility fell on S/L Speedy.

While the show was going on the weather that had closed Karachi now struck Jiwani with extreme violence. Four or five inches of rain fell in as many hours. The only inconvenience to most of us was wet feet paddling back to our billets. All the RAF buildings stood up alright and kept the rain out. After a few drinks in the officers mess the Imperial Airways Station manager with the Waters sisters and 'Stainless Stephen' and others set off in his station wagon for the luxury of the Imperial Airways hotel. The rain was still falling. About mid-way between the two camps the station wagon ran off the road and became thoroughly bogged down, up to the axles. In view of the weather and all the circumstances they decided to stay in the car until daylight.

Next morning was clear sky and sunshine, Karachi signalled they were open for business. Our aerodrome, which was only hard sand, we kept closed until about 15.00 hours when due to the good natural drainage, parts of it had dried out enough for aircraft to take off. All our unexpected visitors drifted away and a gang of airmen went and dug out the station wagon for Imperial Airways.

There was a cinematograph projector on the camp but it did not work. Various 'experts' amongst the airmen had tried their luck with no success. About January 1944 a fresh airman came onto the strength, he heard about the projector and had a go at it. He found nothing wrong with the electrical or mechanical arrangements but he realised a small mirror that was a vital component was missing. Using local material he fashioned a suitable mirror and hey presto, it all worked. Then at two or three week intervals Karachi would send up old films. When a film arrived, in the evening, the airmens mess would be converted into a cinema. As we had only one projector we had a ten minute interval when the reels needed to be changed. This was better than nothing. Now the Americans were on the camp they also had a projector, by joining forces they were able to put on a proper showing.

The airmens mess did not make a very good cinema. The airmen found a sandy embankment and with a little labour made terraces, seats etc and erected a structure to hold the screen. We now had a pleasant open air cinema. American aircraft were then flying through from California-Brazil-West Africa-Middle East-Jiwani. They brought some of the latest releases. So under the black star-studded Indian sky we could sit and watch films that had not been seen in New York or London.

One of these films was 'Dr Jekyll and Mr Hyde' starring Spencer Tracy. I was then twenty six years of age but that film really terrified me, I went back to my billet in fear and trepidation and did not recover for a few days. I have seen that particular film since on the television, although it is very well done I can't now see why I was then so terrified.

Up to 1940 the RAF, for night flying, had used a 'tee' shaped flare path. The flares were laid out in line about a hundred and fifty yards apart. The long upright of the tee would be about fifteen hundred yards long and the bar across the top in proportion. The pilot would land up the long upright of the 'tee' with the row of flares off his port wing tip. This arrangement worked well on grass aerodromes and on desert aerodromes such as Jiwani that had no particular hard runway.

The flares used were known as 'goose neck flares'. Each flare consisted of a galvanised container similar to a gardeners watering can of about five gallons capacity. The spout of the 'watering can' was accurately made and about one and a half inches diameter. Into the spout was pushed a cylindrical wick of a diameter to completely fill the spout, the wick being about a yard long. The wick went down the spout and curled round in the bottom of the can. About three inches of wick was left protruding from the spout and the can filled with paraffin. When a match was applied to the protruding paraffin soaked wick a flame about three inches wide at the base and five inches high was produced by the burning paraffin. This flare could be seen from ten miles away, and could not be extinguished by rain or sixty mph winds. Each flare had attached to its spout by about a foot length of retaining chain a snuffer. The snuffer was a hollow cylindrical steel tube with one end closed, the open end was a close fit on the spout of the can. When the snuffer was pushed over the wick and onto the metal spout of the can the air supply to the wick was cut off and the flame was extinguished. This arrangement seems crude now and it was crude, it was also reliable and effective.

As more and more American aircraft were now passing through they did not appreciate the RAF flare path, they were used to electric flare paths with lights both sides of the runway such that they landed between the rows of lights. They brought in strings of free standing weather proof electric lights, the power for the lights being supplied by an electric generator driven by a small petrol engine. This generator and its engine were mounted on a light-weight tubular metal framework such that it was easily portable.

They laid out their runway lights in two parallel rows with a power supply at the end of each row and instructed us in the starting and running of the engines. They were started by simply pulling a cord, when the engine started that row of lights came on. They also installed on the watch office roof a rotating beacon like a small searchlight about two feet in diameter and tilted upwards. In clear weather the beam from this beacon must have been visible to an airman forty miles away. The power for the beacon came from a similar engine driven generator as was used for the runway lights.

The American signals station was now fully operational. They had installed a separate telephone from their signals office to the RAF watch office and would call and tell us of any aircraft that were expected to land at Jiwani. If it was during the hours of darkness they would ask for runway lights and the beacon to be switched on. One day about 10.00 hours the Americans rang to say they were expecting an aircraft in about a half an hours time. The aircraft was making for Karachi but was running low on fuel and must land at Jiwani. The pilot was enquiring about length of runway, direction of landing etc.

When the aircraft appeared on the circuit it was of a type we did not recognise, big with four engines and of very handsome appearance. This aircraft when it landed had a tricycle undercarriage, all very new, big and impressive. I went down to talk to the pilot. He had flown direct from West Africa and needed fuel to get to Karachi. The aircraft was a new type, a B29. The engines looked enormous, each engine driving a sixteen foot diameter four bladed propeller. So at Jiwani we knew of and saw the B29 before it was heard of in the UK.

The adjutant for most of the time I was at Jiwani was a chap named Beer. He was a great sport organiser, we had cricket matches, football matches and games of soft ball. Imperial Airways staff were always involved somehow. Some evenings it was pleasant to walk on the beach and look for the saws washed up from dead saw fish. The expert at beachcombing was Corporal Berry of the MT section, his home town was Ipswich. He picked up a sawfish saw about two feet six inches long. At parties he would always get the chaps singing 'I've got a lovely bunch of coconuts'.

In the middle of May 1944 a signal came telling me to report to 22 Ferry Control Unit at Allahabad for flying duties. Now it was my turn to pack up my old kit bag and say cheerio to all the chaps at Jiwani and hitch a lift on a passing aircraft to Karachi.

CHAPTER NINETEEN

TRANSPORT COMMAND
MID MAY 1944 TO MID DECEMBER 1945

*FOR LOCATION OF PLACES REFERRED TO IN THIS CHAPTER
SEE MAPS No. 15 (CHAPTER 14) & MAP No. 14 (CHAPTER 13).*

<u>22 FERRY CONTROL</u>
ALLAHABAD
MID-MAY TO EARLY
OCTOBER 1944

<u>No. 9 FERRY UNIT</u>
BISHNUPUR
EARLY OCTOBER 1944 TO
END OF FEBRUARY 1945

POSTINGS WITHIN
TRANSPORT COMMAND

<u>No. 14 FERRY UNIT</u>
AGARTALA
END OF FEBRUARY TO
END OF JULY 1945

<u>209 STAGING POST</u>
AGARTALA
END OF JULY TO
MID-DECEMBER 1945

see over for list of illustrations

223

List of illustrations etc at the beginning of Chapter 19.

Officers of No. 22 Ferry control.
209 Staging Post.
Notes on above photograph.
Lockheed "Hudson".
Beechcraft "Expeditor".

Officers of No.22 Ferry control Unit at Allahabad, July 1944.
On the left of the photograph, front row, Frank Harbord.
In the middle of the front row, W/C. Nolan – Naylon, the unit C.O.
On the right of the middle row are two South African Air Force Officers, note their different style uniform caps. In the back row 3rd., 5th., and 6th.from the left are South Africans.

209 STAGING POST, RAF AIR COMMAND S.E. ASIA

The above photograph was taken about May 1945. The unit was then located at Arartala, approx. 200 miles north east of Calcutta (India).

The purpose of the unit was to deliver replacement aircraft to the forward squadrons. The unit ran a flight of six Hudson's. A Hudson would follow the delivery flights around the forward airfields to pick up the ferry crews and return them to Agartala.

The aircraft in the photograph is a Hudson. Third from the left in the second row (from the front) is F/LT Frank Harbord D.F.M. In the same row immediately beneath the nose of the aircraft, wearing a bush hat is S/Lr. Anderson the unit C.O.

Lockheed " Hudson"   as used by Transport command in India 1944/1945.
Reproduced with kind permission of Comm Squadron Aviation Photos.

Beechcraft "Expeditor" of the R.N. Similar aircraft were used at 209 Staging Post at Agartala in 1945. The aircraft used by the R.A.F. were painted in the normal wartime camouflage colours.

PHOTO COURTESY - M.A.P., ASLACKBY, SLEAFORD, NG34 OHG.

On 27th of May 1944 a Hudson of 353 Squadron landed at Jiwani for fuel on its way to Mauripur (Karachi). It was flown by F/O Gabitas and next morning conveyed me to Karachi. This was all familiar country to me now as I had been in India over two years and was well acclimatised. Flying Control told me they had been notified a Liberator was taking off for Allahabad that night, to be precise at 0200 hours on the 29th of May 1944. The pilot agreed to me being a passenger.

At 01.30 hours on May 29th I loaded my kit onto the Liberator and at 0200 hours, dead on time, the Liberator took off and headed for Allahabad. The flight took five hours. The waterproof fabric engine covers were stowed in the Liberator's bomb compartment. They made a comfortable bed for a passenger, for most of the flight I was asleep.

Allahabad is about four hundred and fifty miles west north west of Calcutta and was very hot in May and June 1944.The CO of number 22 Ferry Control Unit was W/C Nolan-Naylan. The unit was engaged in delivering new aircraft from Allahabad to operational squadrons in the forward areas. These aircraft were mostly Beaufighters, Mosquitos, Spitfires, Hurricanes and Thunderbolts.

To get the delivery crews back to Allahabad the unit had a flight of eight Hudson's. New aircraft were flown into Allahabad by another Ferry Unit, probably based at Karachi. Their pilots/crews would then return to Karachi, leaving the aircraft at Allahabad. Every afternoon 'allotments' would be telephoned to Allahabad from Air Headquarters in Delhi. 'Allotments' would specify which aircraft type and number was to be delivered to which squadron and where the squadron was located.

Every afternoon an officer would be detailed to sit by the telephone to receive the 'allotments' when Delhi telephoned. This was a very tedious duty on an afternoon when the temperature would be about 120 degrees in the shade. The telephone had to be manned from 13.00 hours to 17.00 hours by which time the individual doing the 'manning' was just about flaked out by the heat. The telephones in those days were not that clear, to ensure the 'allotment' was correctly received involved much requesting of repeats, shouting and spelling out with the aid of phonetics.

In the evening the flight commander would make out a programme for the next day, detailing which pilot/crew to which aircraft and where to deliver in accordance with the 'allotments'. If six aircraft were to be delivered each one to a different aerodrome the collecting Hudson would need to prepare a 'circular' flight plan to avoid going over the same ground twice. If the six aerodromes were far apart, say one was to Imphal in the north and another to Cox's Bazaar in the south both about seven hundred miles form Allahabad and about three hundred miles from each other, the Hudson could not get to them all during daylight hours.

On a day when the 'allotments' were similar to the above two Hudsons would be needed, on some days even three. The Hudsons we used were 'demilitarised', having had the turrets and suchlike warfare ironmongery removed. The Hudson was ideal for this work, it had a good eight hours endurance, we could land and pick up passengers without stopping engines and could usually get back to Allahabad without refuelling.

About the first trip I did on the Hudson flight was to fly to Bishnupur (Bishnupur is about seventy miles south of Asansol where I was with 60 Squadron in the summer of 1942) to pick up a funeral party. A Mosquito had pranged at Bishnupur a couple of days before, killing both crew members. We landed at Bishnupur and loaded the two coffins into the Hudson. Then the padre and a firing party with rifles and blanks to fire over the graves. We then took off and flew them to Asansol which was the nearest British Military Cemetery. At Asansol they were met by road transport to carry them to the cemetery.

The composition of the burial party is laid down in regulations according to rank. These two chaps were both flying officers, I have no doubt the funeral party comprised the correct number and rank of officers, the prescribed number of sergeants and other ranks. Rupert Brooke got it about right in his poem 'The Dead':

> Blow out, you bugles, over the rich dead!
> There's none of these so lonely and poor of old,
> But, dying, had made us rarer gifts than gold.
> These laid the world away; poured out the red
> Sweet wine of youth; gave up the years to be,
> Of work and joy, and that unhoped serene
> That men call age; and those who would have been,
> Their sons, they gave, their immortality.
>
> Blow, bugles, blow! They brought us, for our dearth,
> Holiness, lacked so long, and love and pain.
> Honour has come back, as a king, to earth,
> And paid his subjects with a royal wage;
> And nobleness walks in our ways again;
> And we have come into our heritage.

Parties of airmen were sent to the hill stations during the hot weather for ten day spells to benefit their health. Up in the hills they had a chance to get rid of their 'prickly heat' (an unpleasant skin rash) and other minor health problems. Indian railways laid on special trains for these parties and there had to be an officer in charge of the train. For one of these trips I was appointed 'officer i/c train'. It was an interesting experience. The airmen were all on their best behaviour. We were on the train for about forty eight hours. The military set up field kitchens at certain stations where the train would stop for a couple of hours at meal times. The last forty miles of the trip up into the foothills was by motor transport. I cannot now remember where we left the train or which hill station we went to.

It was at this hill station that I had my only experience of leeches. We were told about leeches in lectures from the MO. If we found a leech had attached itself to us it must not be brushed off as its mouth parts would remain in the flesh and cause septicaemia. The recommended means of getting a leech off you was to apply tincture of iodine to the skin above where the leech had attached itself such that the iodine ran down into the leeches mouth. The taste of the iodine would cause the leech to let go and fall off. Another way was to apply the hot end of a lighted cigarette to the leeches body.

One evening I felt some irritation around my right ankle. When my sock was removed there was a leech. It had been there some time and was so bloated with blood it was about the size of a golf ball. It had had its fill of blood and had fallen off but was retained in my sock. Before it attached itself to me it would have been about the thickness of a matchstick and about an inch long. It would have got onto my ankle through my sock when I walked through some vegetation. Airmen often carried a phial of iodine with them as it could be used for an antiseptic as required, it could also be used to purify water in an emergency.

So the airmen had their ten days up in the hills enjoying a reasonable climate. Then it was down to the railway station, on to the train and the journey over the parched plains of northern India back to Allahabad.

The Ferry Control Unit at Allahabad not only delivered new aircraft, they would also collect aircraft and move aircraft for any reason as directed by Air HQ in Delhi.

We delivered new Beaufighters from Allahabad to Colombo (Ceylon) to 22 Squadron which was being re-equipped with Beaufighters to replace their Beauforts. After delivering the Beaufighters we flew the old Beauforts to a Repair and Salvage Unit in northern India. The huts on the camp at Colombo were thatched with leaves from banana trees. On one of these trips we brushed past a monsoon cumulo-nimbus cloud. The turbulence was violent, from four thousand feet we were thrown to two thousand feet and the wooden edging around the wing tips was splintered such that it looked like tightly bound bundles of straw.

On the first of October 1944 I took off in a Vultee Vengeance (American dive bomber) to deliver it to Jodhpur. The pilot was W/O Veales, a Canadian. In the region of Agra the engine died, we made a wheels up landing in a flat smooth dried up river bed. A number of curious villagers came to see what had happened. From these villagers we learned the location of the nearest police post with a telephone. After we had been on the ground half an hour W/O Veales went off to find the telephone to contact the RAF, I stayed with the kite.

All the villagers walked about bare foot. The men wore just a loin cloth, the women with a length of cloth wrapped around them and draped over their heads. The children wore no clothes at all. Lubricating oil was dripping from the damaged engine. One of the villagers asked me if he may please put some of this oil on his knees as he was suffering from rheumatics. He caught some drips in the palms of his hands and massaged it into his knees.

After we had been on the ground about an hour an American Curtis-Wright 'Commando' flew over. He saw the Vengeance on the ground and came down to have a look. I waved my arms and moved about such that he could see I was alright. He made a circuit and came back at a height of about twenty feet, throttled back, and threw down to me the first aid kit in a canvas satchel as carried in all aircraft. Although the first-aid kit was not wanted it was a most kind gesture. Unknown to me he was also sending a signal to Jodhpur.

About half an hour after the 'Commando' flew away W/O Veales came back accompanied by a local policeman who was authorised to take charge of the aircraft. Also contact had been made on the phone to Air HQ in Delhi so the situation was known and we were free to make our way to Allahabad. We must have walked to the nearest railway station. As it had been a very hot hard day we had a cold shower under one of those elevated water towers used for putting water into the steam engines. The 'Ferry Aircrew Pass' we carried got us priority tickets on the railway to Allahabad. About a week later we found out that the engine on the Vengeance had died due to a fractured fuel pipe.

Allahabad I always imagined was a British Army base in peace time. On the outskirts of the town was located a fort. This fort was very extensive and very strong and secure. It was built of red brick, probably after the mutiny of the 1850s as a strong point able to withstand prolonged siege. In 1944, located within this fort was an 'officers shops'.

In areas of India where there was a concentration of military personnel usually an 'officers shop' could be found. These shops were like military clothing stores where officers could buy items of uniform clothing, boots, bush hats, equipment etc for cash. No long and tedious form filling, requisitions, countersignatures etc were required. These shops enabled officers to replace lost or worn out items of kit with a minimum of trouble.

To get to the officers shop in the fort at Allahabad one had to get past the guard room and sentries and other security obstacles. On arrival at the counter where the transactions took place a notice as follows was displayed:

'As man to man is so unjust
I do not know which one to trust
I've trusted many to my sorrow
So prove your identity or come tomorrow'.

You were required to produce documents, including an identity card with a photograph to prove who you were, if you did not have these or if they were not exactly in order no transactions could take place.

About the middle of October 1944 some re-organisation took place, although I never moved I now found myself on the strength of No. 9 Ferry Unit. A day or two later I did move to Bishnupur with all of the Hudson flight. This flight now became a separate unit under the name of the Ferry Convoy Flight. I most remember Bishmapur at that time for the rat infested huts we lived in. The rats ate the buttons off shirts and bush shirts, they ate the bristles off shaving brushes. They took away tablets of soap and shaving sticks. Leather shoes and boots were also on the menu. As well as rats eating the uppers of shoes and boots termites would come up through the floor and chew through the soles, ants were everywhere.

So at night all gear had to be put away in sheet steel trunks, the four legs of the bed had to stand in tins of paraffin to keep out ants and bed bugs. The mosquito net was suspended from bamboo rods tied to the bed legs, the only way for insects to get onto the bed was either by flying or swimming through the paraffin. Our camps were always plagued by pariah dogs, always known to us as pye-dogs. Attempts were made to reduce their numbers by shooting them with the .303 rifles. Pye-dogs were so tough they would often continue running away although we knew they had been hit by a .303 bullet, a 'Sten' gun at close range was more effective.

We carried on flying the Hudsons or anything else that came up. I flew with the unit CO, F/L Beatty a Canadian; after he was posted I flew with John Mather who took over. One day when taxying a Hudson on the taxi-track the aircraft swung off at ninety degrees on its own volition. After coming to rest John tried again, engines and brakes perfect. He taxied up to the engineering section and told them what had happened. While we watched they jacked up that leg, took off the wheel and exposed the internals of the brake. They were multi plate brakes, about twenty-five steel plates splined to the axle and twenty five brass plates splined to the wheel hub. These plates were arranged alternately and when the brake was applied they were squeezed together by hydraulic pressure.

The flight sergeant took off each plate carefully and examined it for wear and distortion. All the plates and all other components were within the specified limits. Put it all back together, all perfect. A few days later a similar fault and again a third time. No reason could be found and things began to be said about John's exposure to the sun. A few weeks later all was explained and John's reputation was restored. The hydraulic pressure was delivered to the brake by a flexible hose of about twelve inches length near the brake such that the telescopic shock absorber could operate. An especially bright young airman realised that when the undercarriage was compressed it caused the flexible hydraulic pipe to kink, this caused sufficient pressure on the brake side of the kink to cause the brake to lock on. Adjustment to the fixing of the hydraulic pipe solved the problem.

One of our navigators was a shot-putter with an international reputation. He had training sessions in the evenings every few days. We all went along for tuition. How it was that he had a sixteen pound iron shot to hand I don't know, I can't imagine he carried it about in his kitbag. As he had it we all benefited by it. Also there was an

American army 'Indian' motor bike that did not seem to have any particular owner. We all had a go at riding that. It had a foot clutch and a hand gear lever. I remember it was very smooth, powerful and luxurious.

Bishnupur also had a camp cinema, I did go to it a few times but can't now remember the names of any of the films. So things went on at Bishnupur as we approached the end of 1944. Christmas day was a special day. As is the tradition in the RAF the officers wait on the airmen at dinner time. Whether the airmen think this is a good thing or not I don't know. We all had a jolly time. Flying did go on on Christmas day as usual.

About January 1945 the mess treasurer collected money in payment of mess bills in the mess in the evening and put the money into a metal cash box with a locked lid. When the bar closed about 23.00 hours the cash box was missing. An extraordinary mess meeting was called the next day. The cash box had been found broken open and empty. At the meeting the PMC outlined action that could be taken: report the matter to higher authority, this would mean bringing in the RAF police (the unmitigated bastards) and the local police. Alternatively we could keep the matter 'in house. He left it to the mess to decide.

All the mess members were satisfied nobody in the mess would do that, nor any of the local Indians employed in the mess. All the mess members agreed to pay their bills again and keep the matter in house. So that was how that was resolved. In March 1945 rumours began to circulate that we were going to lose the much liked Hudson. It was the ideal aircraft for our job. It was rugged and powerful, would take fifteen passengers with kit, no trouble. The aircraft had engines of over a thousand horse-power each, either Wright 'Cyclones' or Pratt & Witney 'Twin Wasps'. One of the more horrifying rumours was that the Hudson would be replaced by the Beaufighter, which all the airmen involved considered totally unsuitable.

Why the higher authorities wanted to change the Hudson when it was so ideally suited to the job we didn't know. In March 1945 another move for the unit was announced, we were to leave Bishnupur and move to a new base at Agartala. Agartala was about two hundred miles north-east of Calcutta. In 1942 when 60 Squadron was based at Asansol, Agartala was often used as a forward landing ground.

I carried on with my spare time job (flying being the main job) as officer in charge of secret and confidential documents. Any transactions regarding these documents were carried out by the officer i/c with other officers signing as witness's. Any movement of documents was made by 'the safe hand of an officer'. Everything was checked, double checked, signed for by the officer i/c.

At any time specialist officers from 'Wing' or 'Group' could descend on the unit and ask for a 'muster' of secret and confidential documents. Any discrepancy found would lead to a court-martial for the officer i/c. From time to time documents and codes were replaced by newer versions. The outdated copies had to be destroyed by fire. I would make a little bonfire and ask a colleague to witness what I burned and to sign the certificate and to stamp all over the ashes.

About April 1945 I found myself one day alone and stranded at Alipore airfield near Calcutta. How it came about that I was there has faded from memory. A Dakota came on the circuit. There was some excitement in the watch office, the ambulance and fire tender moved forward. The Dakota landed and was pursued along the runway by the ambulance and fire tender. The Dakota carried the markings of the Free French Air Force.

On the circuit a vulture had come through the windscreen and hit the pilot in the face. The second-pilot, who was uninjured, took over and made the landing. The medical people found that the pilot had been killed by the impact.

An hour or two after the accident to the French Dakota, on enquiring at the watch-office, I learned that an American B17 parked near the watch-office would be leaving for Agartala in about an hours time.

The pilot of this aircraft agreed to take me as a passenger, this turned out to be an interesting experience. The crew came aboard and started up an auxiliary engine which was fixed to the floor about the middle of the fuselage. The engine was about the size of a single cylinder motor cycle engine of the day and drove an electrical generator to provide power to start up the main engines. When all the main engines were running the auxiliary engine was shut off.

All around the inside of the fuselage were guideways to carry the long belts of half inch calibre ammunition feeding the many guns from which the aircraft derived its name of 'Flying Fortress'.

The rumours about replacing the Hudsons with Beaufighers turned out to be false. Instead we received a couple of Expeditors in the middle of April 1945. The Expeditor was the same configuration as the Hudson but less than half the size and with engines of about three hundred horse power each. They were a 'civilian' aeroplane for women and children, not made for the rough treatment meted out by real service airmen in a war zone. They would carry about six passengers sitting upright in seats. From memory the Hudson had no seats, service airmen did not need them, they would make their own arrangements.

So we all carried on doing what we did using the Expeditors when appropriate. This was about the time when the tide of war began to turn in our favour. Germany gave up in May. In the Arakan north of Akyab the Japs cut off a part of the British Army and waited for it to surrender. This tactic had always worked well for them in the past. This time it did not. The army formed a square with defences on all four sides. Into this square the Dakotas dropped all the food and ammunition that was needed. The army in the square had sufficient material to push the Japs back, this combined with other units pushing from the north towards the square caused the Jap line to break and the square was relieved. At this time the British and Americans had sufficient fighters to beat off any Japanese attempt to interfere with the supply dropping Dakotas.

In the north Imphal, which was also besieged, was also supplied by air. After being defeated in a face to face fight with the British at Kohima the 'march on Delhi' collapsed. Constant pressure by the British began to push the Japs back towards Rangoon.

In June 1945, with John Mather in an Expeditor, we landed on the all-weather airfield at Akyab; a little bit over two years since our attempt to capture it when I was on 60 Squadron. The unit received more Expeditors and we used these now more than Hudsons. The 14th Army continued its push towards Rangoon despite the monsoon. We all felt we were now winning. Mandalay was captured. We continued with whatever came up, mostly flying the Expeditors, occasionally Hudsons and Dakotas. About the end of July Rangoon was captured and many British POW's were released from Rangoon jail. Amongst these prisoners to our amazement was Jim Coppin. Jim was W.Op/AG on a 60 Squadron Blenheim that was seen to crash on the runway at Akyab about June 1942. When the aircraft was shot down it burst into flames and the pilot and observer were killed, how Jim got away with his life and then survived about three years as a prisoner of the Japs is always a source of wonder.

A few weeks after Rangoon was captured, John Mather and myself were at Mingaladon with a Dakota to bring out twenty-four sick or wounded stretcher cases and fly them to hospital in Calcutta. To carry the stretchers the Dakota was fitted up with a harness of webbing. This harness of webbing had loops stitched in it to accept the handles of the stretchers. On the port side of the main fuselage a dozen stretchers could be looped into the webbing harness. The stretchers were fitted into the harness lengthways with the patients head towards the front. To get so many in they were laid side by side and one above another. Similarly on the starboard side, leaving a walkway down the middle for the medical orderly.

Before the aircraft was loaded we consulted the met report, clear sky with unlimited visibility at Calcutta, some weather over the Burmese hills. This appeared OK so the stretchers were loaded and with two medical orderlies on board we took off. We soon realised the weather was worse than we expected. To get over it we had to climb higher and higher. We had to bring in the superchargers and go onto oxygen as we were at over twenty thousand feet. The medical orderlies covered their patients with blankets and arranged their oxygen masks. I don't remember details of the oxygen supply but it must have been so as we went up to twenty three thousand feet.

We called the airfield at Alipore (Calcutta, where we were to land) they assured us clear sky and unlimited visibility. Soon after this we saw a hole in the clouds with the green ground below. This was an unexpected lucky break, John reduced the power and we made a spiral descent through the hole, levelling out in the clear at about two thousand feet and steering west. We crossed the coast, ran through some rain, and about five miles out to sea broke out into glorious sunshine with the clear sky and unlimited visibility as promised. We climbed to a comfortable altitude and had a smooth run into Alipore. It must have been a terrifying experience for the chaps on the stretchers.

To evacuate the wounded from the battle zones all sort of aircraft had been rigged up to carry stretchers, such as the American L5 and the British Tiger Moth.

By early August it had been decided that we should move to Mingaladon to be nearer to where the action now was. On August 14th 1945 at 0630 hours John Mather, myself and an advance party of five airmen took off to fly to Mingaladon. We landed at Akyab for fuel then climbed up over the hills and into the Irrawaddy valley to approach Mingaladon from the north. About fifty miles north of Mingaladon the weather began to turn thick. The nearer we approached to Mingaladon the thicker the weather became. There was no way round the weather and when we were about ten miles north of Mingaladon John decided it was not safe to continue and turned away northwards. With fuel gauges reading zero we landed on the old aerodrome at Ywataung.

Luckily for us there was an army signal station nearby and a RASC ration depot. We sent a signal to Agartala and to the RAF station of Magwe about thirty five miles to the north. Magwe replied that roads had been made impassable by floods, they would bring fuel as soon as the flooding subsided. We went to the RASC ration depot and asked for rations. They asked how many men for how many days. As we hoped to be rescued next day we just asked for rations for seven men for one day.

From somewhere, somehow we were in possession of a kettle, frying pan and saucepans. When the army had been advancing down there they had been supplied by air. These supplies had been packed in bamboo baskets and dropped by parachute. Many of these broken and empty baskets were strewn around the area. Somehow there was still a water supply on the aerodrome. With the rations came mepacrine, salt tablets and water purification tablets.

When the last people had gone from the aerodrome they had left behind, still erected, some tents. Also an unserviceable Hurricane aeroplane. We occupied the tents, collected the broken bamboo baskets to use as fuel to cook with and to boil the kettle to make tea. Next morning we went again to the signals station to see if there was anything for us. As there was nothing we drew another days rations and went back to our camp. This became a daily routine.

On the morning of August 16th or 17th the local villagers told us Japan had surrendered. This seemed of little interest and made no difference to our daily routine. The surrender was confirmed by the chaps at the signal unit and the RASC. Our daily routine continued and we never did get any reply from Agartala.

About 1000 hours on August 20th 1945 a Dakota appeared on the circuit at Ywatanng, landed and taxied towards where we were parked. As the Dakota taxied up so a RAF petrol bowser drove on to the camp, the road from Magwe now being passable. Out from the Dakota stepped the Flight Sergeant maintenance from Agartala and a couple of flight mechanics. They had brought with them everything needed to service the Expeditor; oil, petrol in four gallon cans, tools, fully charged spare batteries etc. The crew of the Dakota were three officers, the only name I can now remember is F/O Banks who was the navigator.

It was quicker and easier to refuel the Expeditor from the bowser, when this was done the bowser departed on his journey back to Magwe. When all inspections were completed we all got aboard the Expeditor, started up, ran up the engines, tested the switches, all OK. Taxi out and take off, as we made a circuit we watched the Dakota take off and head for Agartala, we set course for Akyab where we would take on more fuel.

At Agartala there was a relaxation of tension. All Canadian had gone, having been recalled to Canada. The move to Mingaladon was cancelled, we were to stay where we were. Things went on as before but in a more leisurely manner. The atomic bomb was talked about but was beyond comprehension. However bad it was the feeling was that it was richly deserved, considering the 'rape of Nanking', Pearl Harbour, the treatment of prisoners etc. New aircraft continued to arrive from the UK and were distributed to units as before.

One day in September 1945 I was with John Mather at Mingaladon to collect a Dakota having flown in with something else. There was much security in evidence, flags were flying and a raised platform had been set up near the watch office. We learned Lord Mountbatten was on the camp and that he was there to accept the surrender of the Japanese generals commanding the Japanese army in the district.

These generals were flying into Mingaladon. As the place was swarming with RAF and military police we went for a walk off the camp. Not far from the airfield perimeter we came across a large pond and into this had been pushed about half a dozen Japanese 'Tony' fighters. All had their propellers removed and all had suffered deliberate damage and were partially submerged.

In due course the Japanese aircraft arrived, it was the equivalent to a Douglas DC2. It had been given a thin coat of white paint and the national markings had been replaced by the red cross emblem. After it had taken off we went back onto the camp to carry on with our duties. The chaps who had serviced the Japanese aircraft said it was in very poor shape, virtually falling to pieces.

People began to be posted away from Agartala. The Indians were anxious to see the British out of India. We heard talk of the 'air trooping scheme'. This was an organisation to fly military personnel back to the UK in large numbers in converted bombers as sufficient troop ships were not available. Throughout September and October 1945 John Mather continued as flight commander and I flew with him on the Expeditors. The strength of the unit fell steadily, it now had only about one third of the strength it had had in August.

In the first days of November the CO, S/L Anderson was posted away and F/L Livingstone took over. The very existence of the unit was now purposeless. Habit and years of discipline kept the remaining personnel doing the jobs they had done before, the aircraft were all kept serviceable and the camp spick and span. In mid-November John Mather was posted to a squadron flying Dakotas on communications flights between India, Rangoon, Singapore, Bangkok and Hong Kong. This was his choice, although he had been in India for four years he did not wish to return to the UK at that time.

About this time the Americans claimed back all lease-lend equipment. As it turned out the Expeditors were part of the lease-lend agreement, they disappeared back to the USA. The strength of the unit continued to shrink. About mid-December 1945 I was posted to Dalbumgarh to join the air-trooping scheme on repatriation to the UK.

CHAPTER TWENTY

AIR TROOPING WESTWARDS.
MID-DECEMBER 1945 TO
MID-JANUARY 1946

FOR LOCATION OF PLACES REFERRED TO IN THIS CHAPTER SEE MAPS IN PREVIOUS CHAPTERS SHOWING ROUTE WHEN FLYING EAST.

List of illustrations at the beginning of Chapter 20.

Avro "York".
Notes on above paragraph.

Avro " York "

Avro " York ", as used bu R.A.F.Transport Command for air trooping in 1945/1946. The type was created by taking the wings, engines and tail unit (with an additional central fin) from the "Lancaster" bomber and fitting these items to a new fuselage designed to carry the maximum freight and/or passengers.

The particular aircraft in the photograph was used by Lord Mount batten when he was Supreme Allied Commander in S.E. Asia 1943/1945.

The photograph is autographed by Air Chief Marshal Sir Richard Peirse, K.C.B., D.S.O., A.F.C., who held a senior appointment in Air Command South East Asia at that time.

Reproduced with kind permission of Comm Squadron Aviation Photos.

Dalbumgarh was about a hundred and fifty miles west of Calcutta. It was the assembly point and the starting point for the air trooping scheme in eastern India. For aircraft with sufficient range the route to the UK was Karachi, Shaibah (near Basra, Iraq) Aqir (Palestine), Tripoli (north Africa) and Holmesley South five miles east of Christchurch UK. Shorter range aircraft would land at intermediate aerodromes for fuel.

At Dalbumgarh the camp was crammed full of airmen. The story was that a few days of bad weather over France and the UK had caused the whole system to jam all the way back to Dalbumgarh, we just had to sit and wait. The Indian weather in December is quite pleasant, like an English summer, so sitting there was no great hardship except that we wanted to be moving. The RAF policy of constantly moving people about did have advantages as amongst the people waiting at Dalburngarh I met several people I had known on other units, including three from 60 Squadron.

So we sat and waited and the days went by. Christmas 1945 approached, was celebrated, and went on its way. In keeping with the tradition the officers waited on the airmen at Christmas day dinner. I spent four Christmas days in India, one at Jessore (now in Bangladesh) one at Jiwani (now in Pakistan) one at Bishnurpur and the last one at Dalbumgarh.

During the first week in Jan '45 there was much movement in the camp, the log-jam had moved and the Dakotas that shuttled between Dalbumgarh and Karachi began to move again. Those who had waited the longest went first. It must have been say Jan 7th when my turn came. After waiting about five weeks the Dakota moved me into Karachi in as many hours.

At Karachi arrangements had been made for dealing with thousands of airmen in transit. In a hangar they had erected tubular steel scaffolding to support bunk beds five beds high in rows running the length of the hangar. Each row was identified and each bed numbered. At the end of the bunk was space for a kit bag which was all we were allowed to carry, other gear to follow by boat. Similar arrangements were made in other hangars.

I spent two nights in the hangar. As I remember the hangar doors were always wide open for ventilation and the lights were always on. Passenger lists were posted up on notice boards, it was up to individuals to inspect these lists and take action accordingly. The lists specified the aircraft number, type, time of take-off etc. My name came up for a Liberator. At the appointed time the liberator took off and headed for Shaibah.

We landed at the long established RAF aerodrome at Shaibah in the middle of the night. No blackout now, all the apron area floodlit, the war really was over. After refuelling the Liberator took off again into the black night for Aqir (Palestine). From Aqir the Liberator took off empty heading back to Karachi to bring another load.

Another aircraft flew us from Aqir to Tripoli (Libya). Early in the morning of Jan 17th 1946, about 0500 hours we were all standing about on the tarmac hoping to get a flight to England. The airfield was named Castel Benito, and was just to the south of the town of Tripoli. After our raid on Tripoli docks in August 1941 S/L Goode and the Blenheims of 105 Squadron had flown over this airfield in the dusk at low level and received much hostility from the ground.

Two aircraft were available, a York and a Dakota, and would be taking off about 06.30 for the one thousand five hundred mile flight to the UK. There were seats for us all, we were to sort ourselves out and get aboard. By chance I got aboard the York and sat waiting developments.

One of the airmen produced a box camera and made as if to take a photograph of his mates sitting in their seats. Like a jack-in-the-box up sprang a S/L Morris (a radar officer, not flying) and said in an officious manner 'It is my duty to warn you the taking of photographs is forbidden'. This produced a stunned silence amongst the airmen and embarrassment to all the flying officers. These airmen had borne the burden of the mid-day sun in India/ Burma for the past four years, the war was over, there was nothing secret about the York.

Soon after this the crew came aboard. The pilot a F/L DFC said a few words about the flight plan. The weather forced him to fly higher and higher to get over the clouds, something like eighteen thousand feet. We did not see the ground until the north of France where we began our descent to land at Holmsley South (five miles north east of Christchurch).

Stepping out of the York into England again after four years absence was a unique and exquisite experience, only airmen who have had similar experiences can understand, nobody else can have any idea of the emotions aroused. When I left England from Portreath (Cornwall) in February 1942 my age was twenty three years, now on my return my age was twenty seven. The beauty of England on that January afternoon cannot be described. Add to that we were welcomed by a WAAF officer wearing a fleecy overcoat (was it the one P/O Verity had left hanging on the wall at Bicester that night he went out to his death in 1940).

The Dakota that took off from Castel-Benito about the same time as we did in the York needed to pick up fuel in France. Unconfirmed reports said that descending through the overcast the aircraft hit high ground and there were no survivors.

Being on the strength of Transport Command I was required to report immediately on arrival in the UK to the headquarters of Transport Command at Bushey park (Air Marshal Sir Frederick Bowhill). Holmsley South fixed me up with a rail warrant to Bushey Park. The orderly officer at Bushey Park found me a bed for the night. Next morning Jan 18th 1946 the adjutant fixed me up with a ration card, rail warrant etc and sent me on leave for two weeks. Every minute at that time was savoured, every glimpse of the English landscape was to be treasured. The war was over, no need now to carry a gas mask, there was a limitless future.

On Jan 23rd 1946 I was married at St Nicholas Church, Dereham, Norfolk. As we came out of the church a squadron of P51's (Mustangs) came over. Seeing activity around the church they came down low enough for us to be able to recognise they bore the national markings of the USAAF. They flew round for five to ten minutes while all the activity was going on around the church. This was a parallel to that day in the winter of 1939/40 when with 104 Squadron led by S/L Christian we had circled over Exeter Cathedral to salute an unknown bride and groom.

The appointed day saw me back at Bushey Park, after an overnight stay they posted me to number 24 Squadron at Hendon. I well remember arriving at Colindale underground station and walking up the long straight Aerodrome Road to the gates of the RAF station at Hendon. When I reported to the squadron adjutant next day I learned the squadron was to leave Hendon in a few days and would be based at Bassingbourn. As the CO and most of the officers were away and he was busy organising the movement of the squadron it would be most convenient to all if I went away again for two weeks leave and reported to him again at Bassingbourn.

At Bassingbourn the CO was still away. When he came back a few days later he invited me into his office for a chat. The CO was W/C Walter the very same W/C Walter who had been CO of 113 Squadron at Asansol in 1942 when I was there with 60 Squadron. We talked about old times. The squadron was flying Dakota's on communication flights to the far east involving being away for weeks or sometimes months. If I didn't want the hassle and uncertainty of whereabouts he would post me on to somewhere else, plenty of people at that time who had missed the action in the war were falling over each other to get onto the squadron. Obviously the life he outlined I did not want.

This posting to 24 and the month or so I was on the squadron strength does not appear on my service record which is a disappointment to me. 24 Squadron was a famous fighter squadron of the RFC in WW1. Its most famous CO was Major Lanoe Hawker VC who was shot down and killed by the Red Baron. Major Hawker, VC, DSO, he was flying a DH2 in November 1916 when he became the eleventh victim of Richthofen who was flying an Albatross.

From 24 Squadron I went to the Air Crew Holding Unit at Pocklington in Yorkshire. Walking around the perimeter track at Pocklington it was a sad sight to see four engined bombers just standing in their dispersals, derelict. With tyres going flat and rust streaks running from the engine cowlings. In the mess, hand prints on the ceiling. These hand prints would have been put there by young men on jolly evenings when the squadron was not flying. The next evening the owners of the hands that made the prints were perhaps flying in a bomber that did not come back.

CHAPTER TWENTY-ONE

BICESTER, FOR THE THIRD TIME
AND THE POST WAR RAF
MID-JANUARY 1946 TO DECEMBER 1947

FOR LOCATION OF PLACES REFERRED TO IN THIS CHAPTER SEE MAP No.3 (CHAPTER 4)

List of illustrations etc at beginning of Chapter 21.

Photo of medals.
Names of medals.
Officers of No.1 O.A.T.S.
Notes on above photograph.
Letter from Buckingham Palace.
Notes on above letter.
Entrance to the Drill Hall, Stamford.

MEDALS AWARDED TO 52887 F/L. HARBORD, D.F.M. FOR SERVICE IN W.W. 2, 1939 - 1945.

A B C D E F G H

FOR NAMES OF MEDALS SEE PAGE 255

A - DISTINGUISHED FLYING MEDAL.

B - 1939-1945 STAR.

C - AIRCREW EUROPE STAR.

D - AFRICA STAR.

E - BURMA STAR.

F - DEFENCE MEDAL.

G - WAR MEDAL.

H - MALTA GEORGE CROSS COMMEMORATIVE MEDAL.

IMPORTANT NOTE - AUTHORITY TO WEAR THE MALTA G.C. COMMEMORATIVE MEDAL ON THE SAME LEVEL AS THOSE MEDALS AWARDED BY THE CROWN IS GIVEN IN THE LONDON GAZETTE OF APRIL 15th. 1992.

See also page 254

Officers of No1 O.A.T.S., R.A.F., Digby, Feb/March 1947

This caption applies to the photograph on facing page.

Second from the left in the back row is Frank Harbord.

On the left of the middle row (with the bald head) S/L Hanson, the Senior Admin. Officer. Next to him the W.A.A.F. Officer with the double barrelled name of Speed-Rogers. In the middle of the front row the Commandant of the school Air Commodore Mc. Fadyen.

Behind the Air Commodore in the middle row and to his right, is F/L. "John" Peel the accounts officer.

Still in the middle row and on the Air Commodore's left is F/L Nelson, the unit Adjutant.

Third from the right in the back row is the M.O., F/L. "Doc" Dover.

The photograph was taken during the big snow and freeze up in Feb./March 1947.

The Air Commodore is flanked by two Group Captains, the other four men in the front row being Wing Commanders.

BUCKINGHAM PALACE.

I greatly regret that I **am**
unable to give you personally the
award which you have so well earned.
I now send it to you with
my congratulations and my best
wishes for your future happiness.

George R.I.

Flight Lieutenant Frank A. Harbord, D.F.M.

LETTER FROM BUCKINGHAM PALACE

The letter from Buckingham Palace
reproduced on facing page was sent
to me through the ordinary post with
my D.F.M. in 1947. The King was away
on a state visit to the Union of
South Africa and Southern Rhodesia
at the time in the new battleship
H.M.S. Vanguard.
The paper used for the original
letter is water marked "ORIGINAL
TURKEY MILL".

From Pocklington I travelled with about a half dozen other officers to Catterick RAF station in north Yorkshire which was then the 'Aircrew Allocation Centre'. From there I was 'allocated' to Bicester to attend an equipment officers course lasting six weeks.

In May 1946, Bicester was a very different place to the Bicester of November 1939. Then I was acting sergeant, now I was Flight Lieutenant DFM and with six years of active service on the clock. Also I was married and would be 'living out'. We found a flat to rent in Sheep Street. The flat was in a big old Victorian property next door to the 'Crown Hotel'. The 'Crown' was a relic of bygone days, of the days when to get into a 'music hall' you had to pass through a pub. After the music hall days the auditorium had been used as a cinema.

During the war years the pub and its cinema had been very popular with the airmen. In the last weeks of the war some outrage had taken place at the 'Crown' involving Polish airmen. I seem to remember somebody was murdered and the old music hall was destroyed by fire and the pub closed. The flat we had was across the driveway from the 'Crown'. The property we lived in was owned by a family named Taylor, he was proprietor of the local bus company. When we visited Bicester in the 1970s we found the property we had lived in had been demolished as had the historic 'Crown' and the site built over by a Tesco supermarket.

There were about a dozen officers on the course, all experienced wartime airmen, wearing the ribbons of medals and campaign stars. Only two names I can now remember, a F/O Jones a pilot and a F/O Len Jewsbury (or Dewsbury) a W.Op/AG who I remember came from Sheffield. As I wore more ribbons than any of the others they nicknamed me 'the General'.

After the course I was posted as a supernumerary equipment officer to assist the equipment officer at RAF Dishforth (Yorkshire). It was great at Dishforth. The aerodrome was being used as a 'Heavy Conversion Unit'. Wartime bomber pilots were being trained to fly 'Yorks'. Walking on the moors and walking into Boroughbridge on the old 'Great North Road' were pleasant pastimes. Within a week I was posted again, this time to be equipment officer at No. 1 Radio School,

Cranwell. Cranwell RAF station must not be confused with the RAF College which is on the other side of the same airfield. I had the pleasure of dining in the old RNAS mess and looking at the interesting pictures on the walls for two days. Then came a signal to say this posting was a mistake, it should have been to No. 1 Empire Radio School at Debden in Essex.

The commandant at No. 1 Empire Radio School at Debden, near Saffron Walden was Air Commodore Fagin. It was planned to fit out a Halifax bomber with all the latest RAF radio equipment and then take it on a demonstration tour of the empire including Australia and New Zealand. The gun turrets were removed from the aircraft at Debden by the station engineering officer and his staff. The holes left where the turrets had been were faired over with sheet aluminium by the same people to their own design and manufacture. All sorts of spares were obtained and dispatched to RAF stations along the route, I remember an undercarriage leg was sent to a RAF station near Rome.

Although thousands of Halifax's had been built during the war, spares were now hard to come by. The MU's looked on it as an affront if they were asked for spares. However everything was achieved and the planned flight did take place with Air Commodore Fagin in command.

About November 1946 I was posted again, as it turned out for the last time. This posting was as equipment officer at RAF Station, Digby, near Sleaford, Lincs. The only unit on the station was the Officers Advanced Training School (OATS). The Commandant was Air Commodore McFadgen, his deputy was Group Captain Dickens, a relative, it was thought, of the well known Charles. Many officers with the rank of S/L then had joined the RAF in the early war years and had risen through the ranks by devotion to duty, flying ability, courage etc and had been accepted to stay on in the RAF.

OATS was set up to teach these senior officers all the things they would have learned as cadets at Cranwell. As they were senior officers the lecturers had to be senior officers as well, so the place was alive with Wing Commanders and Squadron Leaders. These courses lasted about two months (my guess) and at the end of each course a passing out parade was held with a march past where the salute was taken by a senior Air Marshal, music being provided by a RAF band. One of these courses was attended by S/L Webster DFC, one of the Flight Commanders on 60 Squadron in 1942. As well as the parade and march past a flying display was laid on, the aircraft flying from various RAF stations. It was on one of these displays that I first saw a DH Vampire. We had to arrange for a bowser of aviation kerosene to be on hand to refuel the Vampire.

As well as the station at Digby the equipment section was responsible for equipment at the old American hospital at Nocton Hall and the Operations Room at Blankney Hall. Both these places were now virtually uninhabited. All the barrack equipment on charge to RAF Digby, Blankney Hall and Nocton Hall was accounted for by the Barrack Warden. For purposes of continuity the Barrack Warden was a civilian, usually an ex SNCO. The Barrack Warden at Digby was Mr Hyatt and he and his civilian assistant had been at Digby since 1918 and knew all about everything with regard to equipment held on the station.

Arrangements were made to set up a school at Digby to train Equipment & Secretarial Officers, the school to be a branch of the RAF College at Cranwell. It began to dawn on me that the RAF I had served in over the past eight years had silently disappeared without me noticing. At Digby I lived out in Sleaford. Once a month we had a 'dining in' night in the mess. These occasions were always very pleasant, the toast to 'the King' being proposed by the most junior P/O from the bottom of the table. After this the port was passed a number of times while the guest of honour, the Commandant and various other senior officers made after dinner speeches.

My age and service release number was twenty five. As my officer's number was 52887 I could stay in the service until I applied for release and I could apply for release any time after release number twenty-five were released. To resettle people leaving the service arrangements had been made for them to attend various training courses. To find out about what courses were available I went on a visit to Brampton Grange near Huntingdon. The Squadron Leader in charge there I had known when he was a sergeant at Bicester in 1941. We had a chat about old times and the Blenheims. He then began to fill in the application form, when he came to my number he stopped and said 'Oh, you were a volunteer, these courses are only available to those who were called up'. So that was that.

I applied for release at Digby and it came through early August 1947. I was to travel to Warton, Lancs, to go through the demob machine. Before I left Digby I had an interview with W/C Wass (acting for the C/O) he thanked me on behalf of the RAF for all I had done and shook hands. I was touched by his sincerity after the brush off I received at Brampton Grange.

At Warton I was fitted out with a civilian suit, shirt, hat, raincoat etc. All these items were packed in a cardboard box and tied round with string. I travelled back to Digby carrying my cardboard box of civilian clothing but still wearing my uniform. It was not easy to accept that after wearing uniform continuously for eight years it must now all be discarded. Due to an accumulation of leave my last day of service was December 10th 1947. December 11th 1947 was the beginning of the brave new world.

Entrance to the Drill Hall, Stamford, in the spring of 1997. The old building partly demolished while being converted into flats.

Note the words "Territorial Infantry Headquarters" and the sphinx badge of the Lincolnshire Regiment carved in the stonework above the entrance arch.

Through this archway passed many a youth to fortune and to fame unknown, to be lost to the sight of men in the path of duty.

CHAPTER TWENTY TWO

RANKS OF THE ROYAL AIR FORCE
RECORD OF SERVICE
VARIOUS POEMS

Ranks of the Royal Air Force

AIR MARSHAL

> Can leap tall buildings with a single bound
> More powerful than a steam train,
> Faster than a speeding bullet,
> Walks on water,
> Gives policy to God

AIR COMMODORE

> Can leap tall buildings with a running start,
> More powerful than a diesel engine,
> Just as fast as a speeding bullet
> Walks on water if sea is calm,
> Discusses policy with God.

GROUP CAPTAIN

> Leaps short buildings with a running start
> More powerful than a tank engine,
> Can occasionally keep up with a speeding bullet,
> Walks on water in small lakes,
> Talks with God.

WING COMMANDER

> Leaps short buildings with a running start
> Is almost as powerful as a tank engine,
> Is able to avoid a speeding bullet,
> Walks on water in indoor swimming pools
> Talks to God if special request granted.

SQUADRON LEADER

> Can just clear a small hut
> Loses tug of war with tank engine,
> Can deflect a speeding bullet,
> Swims well,
> Is occasionally addressed by God.

FLIGHT LIEUTENANT

Demolishes chimney when leaping small huts,
Is run over by steam trains,
Can handle a gun,
Dog paddles adequately,
Talks to animals.

FLYING OFFICER

Runs into buildings,
Recognises steam trains two times out of three,
Is not issued with guns,
Can stay afloat with a Mae West,
Talks to walls.

PILOT OFFICER

Falls over doorsteps,
Says 'I see no trains',
Trusted only with water pistols,
Stays on dry land,
Mumbles to himself.

WARRANT OFFICER

Lifts tall buildings and walks under them,
Kicks steam trains off tracks,
Catches bullets in his teeth,
Freezes water with a single glance,
Because he is GOD.

AUTHOR UNKNOWN.

RECORD OF SERVICE

OF

FLIGHT LIEUTENANT FRANK ALFRED HARBORD (52887) DFM

Date of Birth: 12 September 1918

Previous Service

Enlisted as No 581215 Aircraftman 2nd Class u/t Air Observer	10. 7.39
Leading Aircraftman	11. 7.39
Acting Sergeant/Air Observer	25.11.39
Confirmed Sergeant/Air Observer	9. 5.40
Temporary Flight Sergeant	1. 4.41
Temporary Warrant Officer	1. 2.42
Navigator B	23. 7.42
Discharged on appointment to a temporary commission	10. 6.43

continued on facing page.

268

continued from facing page.

Appointments and Promotions

Granted a commission for the emergency as a Pilot Officer on probation in the General Duties Branch of the Royal Air Force	11. 6.43
Flying Officer (war substantive) on probation	11.12.43
Confirmed in appointment	—
Flight Lieutenant (war substantive)	11. 6.45
Released	20. 8.47
Last day of service	3.12.47
Commission relinquished. Retains rank of Flight Lieutenant (Navy, Army and Air Force Reserves Act 1954 and 1959)	1. 7.59

continued overleaf.

269

continued from previous page.

Postings

Reserve Command, Hendon	10. 7.39
No 3 Air Observers School	14.10.39
Station Bicester	26.11.39
No 104 Squadron (attach)	26.11.39—29. 2.40
No 101 Squadron	2. 4.40
No 82 Squadron	18. 5.40
No 18 Squadron	16. 5.41
No 105 Squadron	13. 7.41
No 14 Operational Training Unit	28.11.41
Admitted No 90 General Hospital	4. 8.41
Discharged	15. 8.41
No 13 Operational Training Unit	2. 2.42
No 60 Squadron, India	28. 3.42
HQ Middle East	16. 2.43
No 60 Squadron, India	11. 6.43
Mauripur	-
Jiwani	25. 9.43
No 69 Flying Control Section	9.10.43
No 22 Ferry Control Section	15. 5.44
Dalbungarh	-
HQ Transport Command	13. 1.46
Pooklington	5. 3.46

continued on facing page.

continued from facing page.

271

Postings (Cont'd)

Station Dishforth	3. 5.46
Equipment Officers School, Bicester (attach)	8. 5.46–18. 6.46
No 1 Radio School	29. 6.46
RAF Debden	29. 6.46
Station Digby	26. 9.46
Station Hornchurch	18. 6.47
No 101 Personnel Despatch Centre, Class 'A' release	19. 8.47

continued overleaf.

continued from previous page.

Decorations and Awards

Distinguished Flying Medal   London Gazette   16: 7:43
Air Observers Badge   9: 5:40

Medals

1939/45 Star
Africa Star
Aircrew Europe Star
Burma Star
Defence Medal
War Medal 39/45

P A WILLIAMS (MRS)

See facing page for notes on Record of Service

272

Notes on "Record of Service".

<u>NOTE</u>.   The foregoing 'Record of Service' does contain some errors:

1.   "Reserve Command, Hendon", this should be "No. 6 E. & R.F.T.S. at Sywell, Northamptonshire.

2.   "H.Q. Middle East 16.2.43". This did not happen, I suspect this was my pilots course, notification never reached me.

3.   From mid February 1946 to the end of March (approx.) I was on the strength of No.24 Squadron at Hendon and Bassingbourn.

4.   "Station Hornchurch 18.6.47", this never was.

273

THE SUMMER OF FORTY-ONE

We were young, carefree and raring to go,
Our fears we hid, not letting them show.
To Oulton they sent us to answer the call
"Sink German Shipping" Winston said "give it your all".
So into the daylight skies we flew seeking their ships,
Bombing targets inland on some of our trips.

We flew at nought feet for most of our 'ops'
Skimming over trees, hedges, waves and crops.
At times we flew high with an escort nearby,
Hurricanes tucked in and Spitfires up high.
They called this a "Circus" which meant we were bait,
Saying "Come on Jerry, come up and fight before it's too late".

Their flak and their fighters accounted for many,
For John, Ted, Norman, George and dear old Kenny.
Their friends and relatives at home - oh they grieved,
For the telegram saying "Missing" they had received.
They gave their lives for us here today,
We'll never forget them wherever they lay.

The above poem by F/L. Jim (Dinty) Moore D.F.C. of 18 and 88 Squadron's was read by him at the unveiling of the memorial stone at Oulton in May 1994.

Best Wishes from One Blenheim Boy to Another
Who survived the Summer of '41.

J.W. "Dinty" Moore
ex RAF F/Lt. WOP/AG DFC.
18 Squadron.

274

ALPHA AND OMEGA

When you died my friend,
Had you thoughts of me,
You left the world, when still so young,
A beginning, and an end.
We parted a timeless age ago,
Little knowing what was to be.

We shared adventure, in times so strange,
Horror forgotten with heated blood.
We lived a thousand lives and more,
From boys to men we'd quickly change.
And when you died, alas, un -aged,
The memories followed, in a flood.

With ageing limbs, now I stand,
On the headstoned green surround.
Focused thoughts, reverently fixed,
In this lush, but foreign land.
This farewell is now the last,
A finality, on this hallowed ground.

Fifty years and more you've lain,
In perfect peace, and un - aged,
The years at last have taken toll,
Of me beside the rustic gallic lane,
The breeze that stirs this ancient dust,
Whips up, as limp, still flags, are disarranged.

Unshamedly my tears descend,
To fuse with soil that now, forever,
Encapsulates my memories,
To stay with me to journey's end,
That soon for me will beckon,
As I bid a last goodbye, and links to sever.

Iolo Lewis

Who'll grow old?

Another day, and who'll grow old,
The friend that was, is dead;
How many, then, is that this week?
Twelve, or more, we're told.
At twenty-one our mortality,
Is measured, so it's said.

Another month, and who'll grow old,
The toll still grows and grows,
New faces now appear,
To join the flying fold.
I'm twenty-one, the oldest,
As the icy death wind blows.

Another year, but who'll grow old,
Just strangers around me I see,
Some stay a day, or even more,
Then are buried, shattered, cold.
At twenty-two the odds now shorten,
What future can there be?

Another time, but who'll grow old,
As dark cloud shadows lift,
Farewell dear friends, who lie
Abroad 'neath swaying harvest gold.
Generations come and go,
The years have passed, and swift.

My time is nigh, and I am old,
With countenance to testify,
As winters dig their frozen claws
In creaking limbs forever cold
I am the one who's now grown old,
As comrades young, still distant lie.

Iolo Lewis

Best wishes, and very well done.

Iolo Lewis

276

LIE IN THE DARK AND LISTEN

Lie in the dark and listen
It's clear tonight they're flying high.
Hundreds of them, thousands perhaps
Riding the icy, moonlit sky.
Men, machinery, bombs and maps,
Altimeters, guns and charts,
Coffee, sandwiches, fleece lined boots,
Bones and muscles and minds and hearts,
English saplings with English roots
Deep in the earth they've left below.
Lie in the dark and let them go.
Lie in the dark and listen.

Lie in the dark and listen
They're going over in waves and waves.
High above villages, hills and streams,
Country churches and little graves,
And little citizens' worried dreams.
Very soon they'll have reached the sea
And far below them will lie the bays
And cliffs and sands where they used to be
Taken for Summer Holidays.
Lie in the dark and let them go.
Their's is a world we'll never know.
Lie in the dark and listen

Lie in the dark and listen.
City magnates and steel contractors,
Factory workers and politicians,
Soft hysterical little actors,
Ballet dancers, reserved musicians
Safe in your warm civilian beds.
Count your profit and count your sheep,
Life is passing above your heads.
Just turn over and try to sleep,
Lie in the dark and let them go.
There's one debt you'll forever owe.
Lie in the dark and listen.

A poem
attributed
to
Noel Coward

277

REQUIEM

My brief sweet life is over

My eyes no longer see

No Christmas trees, no summer walks

No pretty girls for me

I've got the chop, I've had it

My mighty 'ops' are done

Yet in another hundred years

I'll still be twenty - one.

The poem "Requiem" was written by R.W.Gilbert and read out at the unveiling of the memorial stone at Oulton in May 1994 by S/L.Payne of 88 Squadron.

FOR JOHNNY

Do not despair
For Johnny - head - in -air;
He sleeps as sound
As Johnny underground.

Fetch out no shroud
For Johnny - in - the - cloud;
And keep your tears
For him in after years.

Better by far
For Johnny - the -bright - star,
To keep your head,
And see his children fed.

John Pudney, 1940.

Crest of number 18 Squadron
Royal Air Force.
Squadron motto "Courage and Faith".

OULTON, MAY 15th 1994.

Four airmen of 18 squadron R.A.F., OULTON, MAY 1941.

FRANK HARBORD, GEORGE MILSON, JIM MOORE, ARTHUR KIRK.

Poppy shower tribute as veterans honour air heroes.

Poppies showered from the sky as war veterans remembered 300 airmen who gave their lives for their country.

A light aircraft flew low over a disused base that once launched daytime bombing raids and secret radar-jamming planes.

The Piper Cub dropped paper poppies on to guests at RAF Oulton near Aylsham as they unveiled a memorial to their wartime flier friends who never came back — many from the daylight bombing raids.

Among the dead was Flying Officer "Staff" Sinclair, whose widow Eileen Boorman worked tirelessly with her brother Martin Staunton for more than three years to provide a fitting tribute to Staff and his fallen colleagues.

The radio operator's Fortress plane mysteriously exploded over the Elbe estuary while on a radar-jamming raid to Hamburg.

Yesterday was a day charged with emotion for hundreds of ex-airmen and their families as they revisited the base.

A morning service at Blickling church saw a book of remembrance, containing the names of all the dead from the base, dedicated in front of a packed congregation of veterans and guests.

In the afternoon the marble memorial was unveiled at the airfield, now home for crops and turkeys.

Mrs Boorman, from Sussex, whose husband went missing just three months after they married, said: "It has been more than worth the effort. We have had such help from the people of Norfolk."

RAF Oulton was opened in 1940 and continued in service until 1947. It had the rare distinction of its officers being the last group of people to live in historic Blickling Hall.

Liberator and Fortress bombers from Oulton, fitted with "dustbin and clothesline" bits of electronic gadgetry were used as radar-jammers.

And one of the most famous sorties was Operation Oyster, when Boston medium bombers from 88 Squadron led a raid on the Philips radio factory at Eindhoven.

Report courtesy of "Eastern Daily Press" May 16th 1994.

A booklet on R.A.F. Oulton is available from
Len Bartram on (0263) 861319.

Photograph (reproduced courtesy V.W. Howard) shows the legend on the memorial stone at the cross roads a few hundred yards north of the village of Oulton Street, Norfolk.

"Yet all shall be forgot ..."
Fifty-eight years on, Frank Harbord stands again near the sergeants
mess at Watton in the summer of 1998 (See page 84 for original view
of the sergeants mess). Access to the old aerodrome was kindly
arranged by Mr. Julian Horne of the Wartime Watton Museum, he is
on the left in the picture.

Note the derelict condition of the building, the boarded up windows,
the over grown unkempt gardens etc.
Photograph courtesy J.M. Harbord.